A History of
Irish Fairies

Ann Ferguson

CAROLYN WHITE

A History of Irish Fairies

THE MERCIER PRESS
Dublin and Cork

The Mercier Press
4 Bridge Street, Cork
25 Lower Abbey Street, Dublin 1

ISBN 0 85342 455 1

For Bob and Irene

CONTENTS

I

GENERAL FAIRY INFORMATION

What is a Fairy?

'Fairy' is the generic term for all creatures, mistakenly called 'supernatural', who are neither in God's nor the devil's service. Fairies inhabit most countries of the world, but each nation has its particular cultural group. Irish leprechauns, Scottish brownies and German kobolds are all fairies, all independent of religion and quite natural in movement, taste and manners.

In Ireland two distinct fairy types exist—the trooping fairies and the solitary fairies. The trooping fairies are to be found in merry bands about the hawthorn tree or at feasts in gilded fairy palaces. They delight in company, while the solitary fairies avoid large gatherings, preferring to be left by themselves and separate from one another. The trooping fairies (the chief concern of Part I of this book) are the major and presiding residents of fairyland; but the solitary ones have greater interest in mortal affairs and hence are generally more familiar to us.

Irish fairyland exists now. It has always existed alongside mortal borders. And there has always been considerable intercourse between the two realms, although the traffic has diminished in modern times. But although few mortals have the ability any more to see those of fairyland, fairies still live in immortal good health and will yet manifest themselves to those sincere of belief and simple and passionate in nature.

Fairy Names

Faery or fairyland is the world in which fairies reside. Some say that the word 'faery' means magic, but that is because, to most mortal eyes, the world seems unreal and lawless. By fairy standards the land of faery and its ways are natural and orderly. 'Faery' is merely a descriptive term with which mortals acknowledge the living land and extension of immortal beings called fairies.

Fairies exist all over the world. In Persia they are called Peri, in Greece Fata or Destinies. In Provençal they are Fada, in Spanish Hada. The names all imply fate. In Ireland they are the *sidhe* (pronounced shee), a name they have retained from the ancient days when they were recognised as gods. In a group they are the *daione sidhe* or fairy people; singly each one is *siog* (sheogue). Some say they get their name *Aes Sidhe* (folk of the *sidhe* hillock or mound) from the large *sidh* or mound in which they inhabit; but others claim that the hillocks got their name from the fairies' habitation of them. The point is still disputed.

Most often the Irish fairies are called the good people or the gentry. In Greece mortals called the blood-thirsting Furies the Eumenides or the kindly ones in the hope that they would not destroy their lands or people. In Ireland the title 'the good people' serves the same function, because the fairies, quick to be offended, must be placated or they might, in a moment of anger, devastate the crops or cause mortal children to sicken and die. What is good for a fairy may be fatal for a mortal; so we hope that by flattering them, they might keep us favourably in mind.

Fairy Disposition

Fairies prefer, above all else, to be left alone. They are at home in their world of intense emotion and delicate sensibilities. Their emotions are unmixed, so that they love and hate with a good heart, their love never palling, their vengeance never anything but deadly and sure. They are beautiful; they own all the treasures of the earth and hence can afford the luxury of generosity. Although they delight in fine wines and feasting, they are never intemperate and hence never suffer from drunkenness or obesity. However, they do not by any means uphold the Aristotelian principle of moderation; rather they have a strong sense of good form and despise vulgarisation. They therefore loathe uncleanliness and any niggardly or petty behaviour. They are aristocrats who take their refinements as the world's norm.

Fairies are passionate creatures who give themselves totally to whatever they do and cannot understand those who do not maintain the same intensity. The present alone exists for the *sidhe*—past and future being no more than pleasurable blurs; therefore their intense moments are never dulled by hopes or regrets or memories of former attachments. What they love or hate intensely today, they may forget tomorrow. They will not wear an old sentiment for nostalgia's sake.

If all the world were faery, the world would be an intense and lively place. But since fairyland and the mortal realms overlap, there will always be a conflict of interests. Fairies, no matter how much they desire it, can never be alone, because mortals have the habit of frequently wandering into their world as they do into ours. Fairies, therefore, have learned to take us for granted. They are not subtle reasoners and therefore cannot comprehend that our manners of living might be alien to theirs. They pick us up and use us as instruments of their own pleasure, because they are careless to consult our wants and needs in such matters. For them the world is a mirror of their desire. Whatever they want, they appropriate; and if the desired object is a mortal and hence protests, they look at him as

9

some curio, which may be turned into an amusement or cast as easily away. Fairies are not evil; they are merely careless. Some might call them self-centred but this is not at all the case. In truth, they do not think of themselves at all, and can never have genuine possessions because they do not divide the world into mine and yours. What the moment brings they embrace; and being immortal they are fearless of consequences.

Since mortals are about and fairies have gotten used to us, the good people do ask certain small courtesies, such as never draining the wine glass at a feast or a poteen flask or a milk pail. If you keep the fire going throughout the night and never throw a pail of dirty water away until you make sure that it will not land on a fairy going invisibly about his or her errands, the fairies will show their gratitude. When well-treated they are generous folk; but they are deadly to those who wrong them.

If one is a mortal it is hard to have anything to do with the good people without getting some kind of mark from them. Their ways are not ours; and they have never been ones for learning foreign customs. Therefore it is wisest for mortals, whose minds are more malleable and bodies more vulnerable, to learn the ways and the doings of the *sidhe*.

Fairies as Gods

The Tuatha Dé Danann, the divine folk descended from the mother goddess Dana or Danu, were gods from Greece (some say, of the Golden race) who came into Ireland enshrouded by a magical mist which hid the sun and their appearance for three days and three nights. Through necromantic arts and superior martial skills, they soon wrested the island from its former inhabitants. But they had not reigned long when the sons of Mil (known as the high Milesian race, from which present-day Irish men and

10

women are descended) attacked. At first they were repulsed by the magic about the island's shores, but the mortal race finally prevailed and an agreement was struck between gods and men. The mortal conquerors would inhabit the earth's surface, while the defeated gods would enter the sea caves and the earth's bowels and make their homes there. Some say that St Patrick himself made a pact with the Tuatha Dé Danann so as to retain the sun-known land for Christian use, but he was obviously centuries too late; upon his arrival the Tuatha Dé Danann were already well adapted to their underworld, although they still had an inclination for visiting their former lands.

When the sons of Mil, that is to say, humankind, came to share the island, they referred to the Tuatha Dé Danann, the gods, as the *sidhe* of Ireland. And to this day, the Tuatha Dé Danann have retained the name. Although now underground and generally invisible to mortals, the *sidhe*, or fairies, have retained their godly powers. When they were known as the Tuatha Dé Danann, they controlled the elements; at their will crops prospered or withered. In fact, although men conquered the gods, they did not enjoy their victory for long. Neither their crops would grow nor their cows give milk until humankind made peace with the gods and appeased them. If fairs were held in the gods' honour, then the immortal ones would protect the corn and milk and land from invaders, at the same time insuring that there would be royal-blooded heroes to lead and tender women to love, merriment in every home and nets full of fish. But if the fairs were not held, humans would have decay, early greyness and young, inexperienced kings. In those early days, mortals were godlike and hence the gods cared for and respected them. But since then gods and mortals have parted ways, the gods becoming indifferent, mortals sceptical. Yet the *sidhe* have always governed the elements, even though they no longer serve mortals well with their power. The *sidhe* still encourage and destroy the seed; as always,

11

they raise and quell the storms.

The fairies are known no longer by the name of the Tuatha Dé Danann and therefore many have claimed that the Tuatha Dé Danann (despite their immortality and divine abilities) died at the hands of the invading mortals. Hence, they argue, the fairies must be of a different race altogether. Yet every quality and power the Tuatha Dé Danann were known to possess can be attributed to the fairies. Not only their name—the *sidhe*—unites them. The Tuatha Dé Danann knew no limits of time, were pre-eminent in magical arts and capable of changing their shapes at will. They not only were guardians of a land of sumptuous plenty in which every manner of sensual, non-cloying pleasure could be enjoyed, but they had individual palaces in which every fancy was indulged. The timelessness, the magic, the shape-changing, the land of plenty and the wondrous palaces are all now in fairy possession.

The *sidhe* (be they recognised as gods or fairies) have been and still are master builders, poets and musicians. In the ancient days, only the Daghda, king of the Tuatha Dé Danann, could perform on the harp the three masterful strains—the first lulling his listeners to sleep, the second provoking them to ceaseless laughter, and the third wringing tears and lamentations. The fairies today possess the Daghda's art. And why should they not; is not the Daghda (although unseen for centuries by mortals) still among them, playing the harp? Are not the *sidhe* as accomplished, as wise and as life-rich as they have been for thousands of years? Humankind may not recall the name of the Tuatha Dé Danann, but the fairies have never forgotten that they are the gods descended from Danu.

Fairies as Fallen Angels

When the christians came to Ireland in the fifth century

12

they endeavoured to discredit mortal belief in the gods called the Tuatha Dé Danann. Since they could not dismiss these potent entities, they declared them to be heroes and thus gave them an historical instead of a divine aura. It being easier to kill a hero than a god, the christians soon declared, not without some regret (for it is well known that St Patrick himself was fond of the tales of the *sidhe*), that the Tuatha Dé Danaan, though mighty and long-lived, were, at last, defunct.

As christianity gained power, the people gradually became convinced of the death of the gods, or rather of the death of the heroes who loved and warred in the glorious ancient days. But if the gods were dead, who then were the entities who inhabited the underworlds and oftentimes fatally brushed shoulders with humankind? These, they were told, were fallen angels. The fairies were regarded as angels who, during the great revolt, were indecisive in support of either God or Lucifer. For their irresoluteness they were cast out of heaven; yet, being too good to be damned and too bad to be saved, they were permitted residence on earth. The fairies were thus stripped of their rightful godhead and given a place within the christian canon. The story, however, is worthy of some attention since, unfortunately, it is generally believed. As God was casting out the indecisive angels, so the story continues, St Michael interceded for them for he feared the heavens would soon be sadly depleted. God tumbled them from the heights, but, out of respect for his saint, never allowed them to reach Hell. Some fell to the earth and made their homes in mountain interiors; some fell into the sea and constructed submarine palaces, and some remained in the air, where, though invisible, they whistle in high-pitched, wind-like voices. In their respective places they have persisted ever since in their irresolute ways. According to the adherents of the fallen-angel story, fairies are, by nature, indiscriminate in their favours and lacking all moral proportion, sometimes helping and sometimes hindering humankind. Fairy activities, never

13

genuinely evil, are dismissed as capricious whims of morally deficient creatures. Necessarily, christianity has a vested interest in this fallen-angel view.

Some christians believe (and these are closer to the truth) that these fallen angels, despite their deficiencies, became the first gods of the earth.

Immortality of Fairies

St Columcille told the fairies they would be annihilated on Doomsday. St Patrick was more generous and assured them they would not achieve Paradise until the Last Day. However, he did not mention whether at that time they would be granted permanent residence; since their bodies are not of substantial matter, they would be incapable of participating in the general resurrection of the body. The fallen-angel advocates, on the whole, argue for the destruction of the *sidhe*. Since fairies are not actually good creatures, they must, by inverse argument, be somewhat tainted, and hence not suited for the continuing joys of Heaven. Some contend that fairies hold a grudge against humankind because humans usurped their rightful immortal seats. Humankind being allowed to populate the angel-depleted Heaven left no room for the irresolute fallen ones, and so they have sought revenge against our race by numerous spiteful acts.

Yet there is no doubt that fairies are immortal. Fairies are gods; and doctrine is too blunt a weapon to destroy them. Blake claimed to have seen a fairy funeral, but that was an English fairy and had not the godly qualities of his Irish cousin. An Irish fairy of one faction may blithely cudgel a fairy of another, and the latter will seemingly be no worse for the blow. Fairies know neither disease nor death; their immaterial bodies are not subject to decay. Nothing physical can prevent them from living forever. And if they thought for a moment that God would not grant them on

14

that last day their rightful place in Heaven, they would destroy this world and all that is in it. God and the fairies have a better understanding of one another than mortals are inclined to believe.

Fairies and Christianity

Some claim that the fairies are afraid of the priest and that they are terrified of the name of God. A man or woman need only say 'God bless you' or cross themselves thrice and they are safe from the fairy power. If ever you see a blast of wind making a great whirl and throwing up dust, say 'God bless them' and throw something at it, for perhaps some mortals are trapped within and these words will set them free. An unbaptised child or one whose mother has neglected her prayers may be swept away at any moment into the fairy realm. A 'God bless you' always defeats the *sidhe*; and surely there are fewer mortals among the fairy ranks since the coming of christianity.

Yet it is not fear but respect that stays a fairy hand at the name of God. Fairies have no wish to run a divine contest between themselves and the Almighty; they take what is available and leave what is His to Him. They are not greedy for divine honours nor jealous of attention. On the whole God concerns Himself more with the activities of humans than ever the fairies do. And if a mortal claims him- or herself to be of God's camp, the good people will politely render unto God His own.

In parts of Donegal and Galway the fairies are believed to be barred from Heaven, yet have the dubious honour of escorting the souls of the human dead to the very gate which is supposedly denied to themselves. Some are more charitable in their beliefs and declare that the fairies are only poor souls doing their penance. For these, fairyland is nothing other than the Limbo of unbaptised innocents or

15

the Purgatory of the penitential. However, fairies serve neither mortals nor mortal conceptions of what their activities should be; only those who fear knowledge of fairyland attempt to graft it onto other realms.

Although many a priest has declared fairies to have no souls, there is sadness and not anger in his voice. On the whole christianity prefers to maintain good relations with the fairies for the very reason that, as the great Irish poet wrote, God is all the nearer when the pagan powers are not far away. Raftery, the itinerant poet, consorted with fairies and died with angels. Father O'Flynn lived with the fairies for a hundred and one years and when he returned from fairyland he was such a holy man that he was made a priest on the spot. His entry into Heaven was proclaimed by melodious fairy voices. And when William Hearne died in America, did not the fairy woman in whose arms he died travel all the way to the Lough in Ireland to exhort his family to read a certain Bible passage for him at the next prayer meeting?

Fairies and the Devil

The story goes that when the fairies were thrown from Heaven some were cast into Hell and became the devil's servants, engaged in tempting mortal souls from their heavenly purpose. The proof for this belief, some claim, is that fairies have cloven feet; and since the devil and the fairies conduct most of their business at night, they must be in league. But, in truth, the fairies are most indifferent to the devil save perhaps for the pooka, who, rumour has it, served Satan on Samhain eve before Brian Boru tamed it. Besides, the continual torments of Hell allow devils little opportunity to disport about the Irish countryside; and the fairies are nothing if not ladies and gentlemen of leisure.

In the ancient days witches, devils and evil spirits, as well

16

as fairies, molested the mortal lands; and humans were not always able to discriminate between malicious and mischievous deeds. All spirits were conveniently lumped together. But since the fairies act from desire and not morality, the principles of evil are as incomprehensible as the principles of good. The *sidhe*, like their familiar friend Death, stand outside of all human moral categories.

Fairy Size, Shape and Number

The giants of the earth of whom the Hebrew prophet wrote may have counted the Tuatha Dé Danann among their number. Mighty gods they were, of gigantic proportions, and humans honoured them as such. But when they went underground and became known as the fairies, human perception of them altered: their heads no longer bumped the heavens but were crowned with diminutive foxglove caps.

The size with which fairies appear to a mortal is proportionate to the belief that the mortal has in them. Fairies have little desire to parade before unbelievers; and since humans have become so arrogant as to believe in nothing greater than themselves, fairies have ceased to be seen as greater than mortal heights. It takes a high-minded mortal to endure the sight of the fairies in all their majestic beauty. A tale written about the cute 'wee people' is one that can be dismissed as fiction. But if fairies were accepted as gods, as awesome gods, they would stand before mortals.

Fairies physically resemble mortals in every way, save that not a one resides among them who is defective in beauty or grace. It is possible for fairies to suffer certain debilities, but the defective ones are rejected forthwith from the community. Some declare that fairies are actually old, deformed and withered and therefore wear lovely but false forms so as to tempt mortals to mate with them; but who can heed the words of the jealous? Yet it is true

17

enough that a fairy can assume any form—sometimes as a furious, fire-breathing horse with eagle wings and dragon tail; sometimes as a rumpled hag, oftentimes as a baby with an old man's face. When in great troops they ride out from their forts, their horses kicking up whirls of dust, they cannot be seen for the dust clouds that surround them, and all that is heard is a loud, monotonous sound like the buzzing of innumerable bees. Contrary to speculation, fairies have neither wings nor cloven feet, being neither angels nor devils.

Being immortal, fairies never submit to autopsy, and hence it has never been determined of what material fairy bodies are composed. Most speculators agree that they are not formed of flesh and bones but of some ethereal but otherwise undetermined substance, like that of a condensed cloud which, being light and thin, enables them to appear and disappear at will. Although these immaterial bodies are subject neither to decay nor destruction, they have all the sensuous advantages of pleasure, and, one supposes (although this has not been recorded), the disadvantages of pain. A Scottish minister claimed that they did not ingest food through the mouth, but rather absorbed 'fine spiritous liquours' like oil and air through the pores into the veins, arteries and vessels, and hence had no need of our messy manner of digestion. But this fine man never saw a fairy lustily attack a mutton at a feast. Their senses, if such they can be called, are splendidly developed; the love embrace or the draught of finely aged wine excites such extremities of delight that few mortals could endure.

Over the generations fairies have rapidly disappeared from mortal view, mostly because of mortal disbelief. Smugly content with themselves, humans have broken the dialogue and put a wall of blindness between the two worlds. And with the loss of the Irish language the fairies probably find few they can talk to. Although the Irish National Schools encourage the language, they have, to some degree, driven fairies from the country because the good people hate to associate with those who have so cluttered their heads with ideas that they are no longer comfortable with their senses and emotions. Thought alienates the good people, while human emotions excite their attention.

Although unseen, fairies still exist and are considered more numerous than the human race; more fairies are added to their number each year and few are ever taken away from them.

Fairy Occupations

Fairies feast, fight, make love, steal mortals and play the most soul-cleaving music the world has ever heard. In fact, they do most things humans do, but with a carefree flair and an effortless perfection. No one has ever recorded whether fairies sweat, defecate or have unreachable itches in the middle of the back; but if it is true that they are composed of an ethereal substance rather than flesh and bones they would not suffer from such debilities.

On moonlit nights the sea fairies ride upon their white horses up onto the land to hold revels with their mountain cousins. All night round the grassy fort or in a woodland clearing they dance to the wild harp, singing their songs in Irish. Occasionally they pass the evenings with card games, while some of the more industrious *sidhe* keep the forge bright all night, hammering iron swords.

Ever since the days when they were called by the proud name of Tuatha Dé Danann, they have delighted in fine horsemanship. Fairy steeds are strong and lean, fleet as the wind, their necks arched, nostrils acquiver. Fire smoulders in their eyes. From rushes or straw, a blade of grass, a fern or a cabbage stalk, the fairies fashion their steeds and with them travel the moon beams and half the world over before day breaks. To Australia and back in an hour is no feat.

And a French princess can be swept off to Ireland and never once think but that she went in a dream.

The fairies can do anything; they can raise the wind and draw the storm, blight the crops or make them abundant, make a healthy man wither and a lame one walk. Some say they are the great agents of all accidents, diseases and deaths in men and their beasts. Sneezing and tripping are attributed to them. When the potatoes are bad, sure the fairies have blackened them. They can strike a man dead on the spot or change him into a horse or a spider or a gilt unicorn.

Some call the fairies the devil's agents because they dry the cows' milk and make her kick the pail, spoil the butter in the churn, steal the eggs, set fire to the thatch, lead the sheep into the bog, blight the crops, make children fall sick and bring rain when sun is needed. But fairies intend no evil; they are completely indifferent to mortals' property and act solely from a delight in exercising their wills.

They are as liable to do good as ill. Overnight a castle might be erected to house a poor man or crops might be harvested and laid in the barn, the turf cut and stacked, the rain given when needed, and the enemy repelled without the lifting of a mortal hand. For the fun of it two fairies took Sean Palmer by boat to America to visit his sister, and they gave some needed tobacco besides.

But the most favoured fairy occupation of all is the fight. With alacrity they divide into warring factions. But over what they contend no one is quite sure. Sometimes a fairy of one clan puts a spell on another or a fairy king steals his neighbour's children to serve as his heirs and thus cause is given. But all in all a good fight is loved for its own sake and a stout blackthorn stick is best where there are foes to be cudgelled. For centuries the fairy clans of Ulster and Munster have indulged in the sport; and many a potato field has suffered from mid-night attacks. A hurling match adequately arouses the fairy blood, but there is nothing as

20

exhilerating as the attack of the clan. Fortunately, immortality enables them ever to continue the sport.

Wanly a mortal man may lie in sick bed, while his fairy friends fight for his health by beleaguering his fairy foes. This action is appropriately called the 'fighting of the friends'. Shouts echo throughout the house in the night; blood besplattered floors attest to the battle in the morning. The man may die but the fairies never forfeit the sport and so the fight continues to and about the graveyard. Small wonder it is that a fairy never misses a mortal funeral.

Fairy Music

The most renowned fairy occupation is the making of such sweet music that only that of the angels singing the praises of Heaven's king can compare. The strains of the fairy harp, which tear the heart with a longing few mortals can endure, are wild and melancholic. Each note excites desire; and since music moves forward in time, unlike a painting which can be contemplated at leisure, no mortal can embrace nor be wholly ravished by its sounds, which tease him then leave him all the more desperate in his frustrated desire to possess. Even though the music rends his vitals, he cannot choose but to listen and exult in his beauteous destruction; and if those strains were to stop, he would die with desire to hear them once more. He loses memory of love and hate, forgets all mortal things and hears nothing but fairy music until the spell is broken and he dies.

Few mortals are equal to immortal desire; yet a rare few have revelled in *sidhe* music and, exultant, brought back those blinding sweet tunes to the mortal realm. Turlough O'Carolan, the last of the great Irish bards, slept one evening upon a fairy rath and ever after the songs of the *sidhe* run wild in his head, and wild and sweet they sprang from his lips. The few fairy tunes we have, like *The Pretty Girl*

Milking Her Cow, are gifts to us from such intrepid eaves-droppers.

'Come with us to the land of delight and rest' play the fairy musicians with fiddles and pipes and drums, and none can resist. They come gliding over fields without bending the grass, crossing rivers without wetting their feet. Being nationalistic, the fairies enjoy praising their home; the music blithely skips from the fiddle, compelling all, man beast and fairy, to see for themselves the joys of *Tír-na-n-Óg*, the ultimate fairyland. Such is the desire, but the delightful destination is not so readily reached; for the music vanishes leaving man and horse standing bewildered in the midst of a stream.

Mortals are always sensitive to the music of the *sidhe*. One morning a mother found her infant son in the cradle lustily playing the bagpipes. She knew at once that it was no child and not her own. Wild through the village the music tumbled and not a mortal could stir nor move his lips for charmed were his will and his senses.

But whereas fairy music oftentimes paralyses mortal bodies, it always animates those of the *sidhe*. Any who pass a rath at night will see them at it in true Irish fashion: their bodies straight as a sapling, but from the knees down they are as quick as a stream. In a ring they dance until the grass and their shoes are worn; and the next morning the tack-tack of the leprechaun's hammer echoes from the hills.

Fairy Locations

Ever since the Tuatha Dé Danann agreed to abandon the sun-ruled land to humans, fairies have made their homes in underground places, emerging only after the moon has ushered mortals to bed. Anthropologists claim that the good people take their name, *Aes Sidhe* (folk of the hillock or mound) from the large earthen mounds, or *sidh*, in which they dwell; but fairies actually have diverse tastes in domiciles and dark, earthen mounds are not in particular favour. Some dwell in the clefts of hills, some in deep mountain caves or in shallow ones near and beneath the sea; some prefer wild strewn rocks and others secluded glens. From humans, fairies have inherited old castles, deserted graveyards, ruined churches and the tombs of ancient warriors. But as humans have become more numerous, fairies have retreated from mortal habitations and sought the seclusion of distant Atlantic islands and unsurpassable mountain ranges. Many emigrated to America to explore new frontiers, but when these diminished the fairies moved on.

Most land fairies dwell within raths (also called lisses, forths and forts) which are circular areas of half an acre or so enclosed by stone fortifications. In the ancient days when they lived above ground as warrior-gods, the good people constructed them as defences against foes and as retreats in which to play their music and create their poems.

From any fort one can see the next a mile or so to his left and another the same distance to his right. Underground passages link them all, so that if a man was brave enough he could walk the length of Ireland without seeing the light of day. It is said that if a man were to sleep within the rath itself, his mortal spirit would be taken away and that of an old Tuatha Dé Danann warrior put in its place; thus would he know all the world's past. But his glory, though intense, would be rather short-lived. For once he has left the rath itself, his new-found knowledge would vanish and his wits dry up and scatter like leaves. Despite all obvious disadvantages, it is safer to enter a rath escorted by the *sidhe* than to stumble in on one's own. An abducted guest will be regally entertained and has the hope of returning with all his faculties intact.

The cave fairies have less intercourse with mortals than their hill-bound, mortal-abducting brethren. In fact they are indifferent to mortal doings, being far more interested in maintaining their reputations for fine horsemanship, which they have held since the renowned times of the Tuatha Dé Danann. Caves are known to make excellent stables. Left in peace (they loathe being disturbed by us newcomers) they are harmless, but their vengeance is devastating and their tolerance questionable. Oftentimes, coming home late at night, fishermen see them traversing the underwater, coral roads they have built to link their cave homes. A wise fisherman will bow them the right of way and make a note henceforth to avoid the area.

When fairies of all locations travel abroad, they most often make camp under a hawthorn tree. Under its branches they feel at home. On May Eve when the blossoms are open, they leave their underground homes to dance wildly about the tree, daring mortals to join them. But May time (or, indeed, any time) humans had best respect the *sidhe*'s sacred tree, for he who plucks a branch will fall helpless to the fairy power.

Fairy Palaces

If one were to walk round a fairy rath three times under the full moon, one might find an entrance to the Sifra or fairy palace of gold and crystal. But it is easier said than done for today the fuchsia and the gorse hedges guard well the raths and hinder the over-curious. Dark hills hide palaces within them, but often a mortal prying about a fairy rath has tumbled through a tunnel and landed within their crystal walls.

Like mortal homes fairy palaces are diverse in construction and arranged according to individual taste. But fairies, being a gaudy lot, prefer crystal outer walls, gilded floors and silver columns. Sea palaces, due to their favourable location, are ornamented with pearls. The numerous great rooms are spacious, never to be traversed completely by mortals save with a fairy guide. Wherever crystal is lacking, kelly green paint prevails, trimmed brightly with gold and red bands and bric-à-brac. Diamonds light up the banquet hall. The finest carpets belong to the *sidhe*, as well as rich wall hangings, carved tables and chairs. And despite their residence within the bowels of the earth, fairies have a curious fondness for window curtains.

No mortal voyager to fairyland has ever adequately described the palaces of the *sidhe*. A 'ten times more beautiful and grand than any house in the world' is the best they can do, so overwhelmed are their senses. And considering the fairy power to wrest anything from mortal hands and earthly recesses with their spells, it is to be expected that the immortal race enjoys a modicum of comfort. In fact with such power they construct palaces in a field in ten minutes. Some say that these palaces consist of such light substance that, having been struck by the spade of an alert, vengeful mortal, they crumble like dust, then gradually fade away. But those who believe in evanescent palaces perhaps underestimate the fairy power to enchant objects and bewilder their foes. What a fairy lives in and what he constructs for a moment's amusement might not be made of similar material. Those who further denigrate the fairies declare their palaces to be nothing but rough, moss-rotten caves, oozing water over a stone and clay floor; only fairy glamour or enchantment, they say, makes mortals mistake dank slime for crystal. But fairies retain their crystal palaces despite some mortals' calumnious nature.

The King, the Queen and the Fool

Every fairy household contains a king, a queen and a fool. For how can one live the good life in a crystal palace with no wise king to rule, no gracious queen to preside over the banquet table and no fool to amuse?

Fairies are royalists. They insist upon a king and queen in every fort and palace. Although the legislative duties of such monarchs may be minimal, they actively lead their fairy court in all social functions. The king initiates the races, the battles and the raiding of mortal lands for beautiful women. The queen orders the feasts and festivities, instigates the battles and surreptitiously sends her dark servant to escort a nursing mother or a handsome young man to her underground home.

King Fionvarra presides over all the western fairies. A lusty horseman, he leads the attack or the race, handsomely astride a great black charger with nostrils red as flames. When not upon his horse, he can be found at table with a goblet of wine in his hand or in bed kissing a lovely woman. Oonagh, his queen, has thick yellow hair sweeping the ground; when she moves her dew-drop dress shimmers like fine mist over her handsome body. But although Oonagh's beauty exceeds that of any mortal woman, Fionvarra fancies the young girls of our realm. He literally charms them, luring them away to dance with him on the fairy rings.

Fairy kings and princes dress in well-fitting green and are inclined to adorn their red caps with fillets of gold. A great golden torc is worn by each king to indicate his rank; for some rule one rath only, while four are worn by the great chiefs of Ulster, Connaught, Munster and Leinster. All are irresistable to young mortal women.

Queens prefer flimsy, shimmery garments to show off their fine forms. The celebrated beauty of Queen Maeve of Connaught meets with every fairy standard: lips like rowan berries, skin like fresh cream, voice as sweet as a well-stroked harp, hair yellow as wheat and sweeping the ground. With such charms, Maeve and lesser fairy queens never fail to capture the hearts (bodies and souls included) of our young mortal warriors.

Every fairy fort houses an Amadawn or fool who keeps well within fairy borders save for the month of June. For

26

eleven months out of the mortal year, he amuses the fairy troop with his heavy clown antics, but in June no fairy fort can contain him when some strange necessity calls him to mortal lands. Wild, half-naked and with an incongruous high hat upon his bull head, he lumbers down our country roads, his short massive body jerking with the violence of his passion.

Not out of meanness but stupidity, the fool lashes out at all he encounters, thus destroying their wits. A boy once saw a fairy fool carrying a shining basin behind his back. He had no time to run before the basin was hurled; when it crashed with a great noise the boy's wits were gone. Some striken mortals never see the fool at all, but their disarranged wits attest to his touch.

Of all the fairies the fool is most to be feared because no remedy exists for his stroke. Even the great fairy doctor, Biddy Early, who could cure all things, found her arts powerless against the touch of the fool. And since he has no wits at all, he cannot be placated nor wittily tricked. One tap from his fist is sure to knock anyone's brains to kingdom come, but a bit may be saved if a mortal says a quick 'The Lord be between us and all harm' before the oncoming blow.

Fairy Clothes and Appearance

Naturally each fairy dresses according to his or her taste, but there are general styles, fashionable now for thousands of years. Ladies prefer shimmering silver gauze for dining at home, and white shifts when travelling abroad in mortal realms—white shifts against the night blackness being known to produce startling effects on mortal sensibilities.

At home fairy ladies and gentlemen enjoy adorning themselves with the treasures of the earth, especially with diamonds and pearls. Somewhere about their persons lies a

27

fillip of gold, on a cap, perhaps, or a hem of a dress. Sea fairies have an easier access to pearls; but land fairies prefer necklaces made from serpents' scales, which they have had to import from England ever since St Patrick chased the snakes from Ireland.

Of course, a great deal of red is worn by the fairies as well as displayed in their homes, for red is the colour of magic, and a great deal of green, for is that not the colour of the fields and the woods and of Ireland herself? Therefore red caps are all the rage in male fairy circles, well-fitting green garments eternally in style. On occasion fairies do sport about in foxglove caps, but mortals have been too quick to cry 'fairy' every time they spy the foxglove and so have falsely attributed diminutive size to the good, but not always so wee, people.

Fairy men and women are as perfectly proportioned as Greek statues, but not so heavy of limb. The bodies of either sex display magnificent features, but mortal writers prefer to dwell upon the female form and hence to devote their descriptions to the fairer sex. Although a few brunettes exist among the fairy court (perhaps from intermarriages with the dark-haired Celts), most ladies have fair hair which would be a disgrace if it did not delicately sweep the ground Such women have a rather sleepy look, with languid bodily movements and a slow feline voluptuousness. Hotblooded women, they think nothing of ravishing a man in an evening's sport or infusing his blood with a fierce war lust. Yet despite the exquisite virtues of brunette and blonde fairy women alike, fairy men have, for centuries, eyed the mortal form, as have the fairy women themselves despite the fine qualities of their men. Perhaps after a thousand-year acquaintance they desire novelty. But more likely, fairies love mortal men and women because, overflowing with love and rejoicing in all beauty, they have the immortal strength to embrace all that is beautiful of both races.

Oftentimes fairies appear before mortals in ancient deformed shapes. But when fairies come to the mortal realms for love, their clothes are tasteful and their bodies straight. They travel abroad most often in troops, and then little is seen of their fine array and splendidly proportioned bodies. They cover themselves with such swirls of dust and straw that not a gold buckle nor a red cap can be seen. A shrill sound like buzzing thrills the air as they storm by with such force that a mortal, knocked down abruptly and dazed of sense, remembers nothing but a great buzzing wind. To see fairies in all their regalia one must be escorted to fairyland itself.

Fairy Food

Fairies prefer to sup on the nectar in flower cups and early morning dew; but since these delicacies are rarely gathered in quantities sufficient to satisfy a fairy appetite, other victuals must be found. Fairies require good meats served on golden platters, and French wines and the finest new potatoes. Chickens and young turkeys, mutton and pasties, butter and cake, all procured by means of pishogues (spells) from the labouring mortals, grace the tables of the *sidhe*. A fairy is too careless to farm, too heedless of all save his pleasure to tend daily to the cows. And why should he when humans provide all in abundance? All lies ready for the taking: a little glamour makes the crop look blighted, and allows the fairies to reap at leisure the harvest.

Although fairies dine well, they never over indulge. Never has one been seen befuddled by drink nor encumbered with a blubbery belly. Although passionate in many respects, fairies are never immoderate at table. Once a mortal invited to a fairy dinner saw an old woman basted and ready for the spit. Horrified at the proposed fare, he fainted, but upon revival discovered the hag gone and a marvellous feast laid on the table. Fairies enjoy playing such pranks on humans over-ready to believe that those with unfamiliar ways must therefore have unnatural appetites.

Many a mortal who tasted fairy food remained forever with the *sidhe* or, once returned to his former land, pined away looking for crystal palaces. Yet many return, for it is from them that we acquire our fairy tales. The secret lies in the salt: fairies never eat it and mortals who but taste of unsalted fairy food have the glamour put upon them, making them forgetful of their former cares. If a mortal carried a pinch of salt (for the fairies are not always gracious enough to provide it) at all times, he would be assured of a good meal, and a good tale to tell when he returned home.

Treasure

All treasure concealed underground and in the hollows of trees, all silver and gold and precious stones darkly glimmering in mountain mines, all cargo locked in sunken argosies and pearls hidden in oysters belong to the fairies. It is therefore small wonder that their palaces are sumptuous and their garments unparalleled. And although fairies freely lavish their goods upon themselves and invited guests, they prefer to keep their treasures within fairyland's borders. Great serpents and water cows settle their slimy bodies securely over undersea treasure; never-sleeping black cats with hostile eyes and knife-sharp claws prowl suspiciously about the treasure stored in fairy raths. Even if a mortal eluded the guardian-beasts, the fairies themselves might attack in awesome, shrieking shapes guaranteed to terrorise all but the most intrepid intruder. The most successful, and least dangerous ploy, is to catch a leprechaun unawares and wrest from him his gold crock. But that, too, as will be seen in a later chapter, has its peculiar drawbacks.

Sometimes, on the rarest of occasions, fairies empty their coffers to a mortal favourite on condition that for seven years he tell neither where nor how he obtained his fortune. But mortals are not serious practitioners of the art of promise-keeping; and fairy treasure itself, being rather sensitive to verbal disclosure, has, once its whereabouts has been revealed, the unpleasant quality of turning into dust or dung in the finder's hands.

Under orders from two old bearded men and an equally bearded crone, John Shea roasted a mutton outside a fairy fort. The cat-guardian, being as susceptible to temptation as a mortal, deserted gold for meat and was instantly strangled by John. Unhindered, the man then entered the fort and removed a basin, a towel and a razor, carefully avoiding the gold treasure nearby. He then proceeded to shave the three, who, with the loss of their hair, also lost fifty years apiece. To reward John they gave him some meat to eat, whereupon he immediately knew the resting place of every gold piece in Ireland. But Irishmen never had much power of keeping a secret; and the three transformed ones soon realised that John was true to his blood. So they slipped him a bit of the mouse broth and his knowledge was taken clean away. It is clear that, despite human protests to the contrary, fairy treasure and mortals have an aversion to one another; and clear, too, are the discrepancies between fairy and mortal values.

II

RELATIONS BETWEEN MORTALS AND FAIRIES

On Encountering the Fairies

The poor, the simple and the sincere are those most likely to encounter the fairies. The fairies loathe qualities they do not possess and appear only to those as passionate and straightforward as themselves. They hold no traffic with the vain and hypocritical. And they shy away from the academic; always the folk and never the scholar record their deeds. When a mortal approaches a fairy he should greet him politely and directly, showing no sign of fear; for fairies have great power over those who are cowards or who suffer from such defects as discourtesy, uncleanliness or dishonesty. Those who share fairy virtues are accepted on fairy terms as equals. Above all a mortal should be respectful upon meeting a fairy queen or king, for nothing inflames them more than a sniggering mortal who laughs at them or regards them as children.

To disbelieve in them is the worst offence of all. Modern man lacks leisure time to encounter the fairies; absorbed in his own affairs, he moves too fast to discover the immortal languor of the good people. It is understandable that mortals infrequently meet the fairies, our own life styles and environments being so different; but it is inexcusable for mortals to be so arrogant as to believe that they do not exist. The presumption is as shocking as Peter Pan's when he declared that the twins did not exist (although they were daily before him), because he could not grasp the concept of twins.

However, whenever mortals and fairies meet, a gentle

affection generally arises between them. Fairies abduct the beautiful of humankind in order to regale them with the wonders of fairyland. They amply reward the generous and high-spirited of our race, and only with good reason or from a genuine incomprehension of human limitations have they ill-treated our kind. Irish spirits do not intend evil, although they do exact a particularly harsh form of justice. Yet since the devil has no influence over the fairy majority, the harm the *sidhe* inflict is never as horrific or deadly as that, say, of the Scottish or Germanic spirits.

But, as many have said, 'it's no use going agin the good people'. Although their vengeance is just, it is a bit heavy-handed for those susceptible to death. Not only do fairies often fail to realise that a mortal's desires are not always the same as theirs, but since they have no interest in the past or future, they have little consideration for mortal attachments, such as a wife's for her husband or a mother's for her child. A mortal should seriously reflect upon these matters before seeking out the fairy kingdom.

Mortals who know and care for the good people show their affection by leaving, in front of the house, cold potatoes or milk or wine or whatever delicacy is leftover. Fairies always rejoice in sympathetic human attention; and they are endeared for life to the men who, without a moment's hesitation, have jumped in and aided them in a rousing game of hurling. If such were always the relations between mortals and fairies, perhaps each race would learn better how to live with each other. Perhaps, as Yeats wished, we would unite with them after our deaths if, in this life, we would keep ourselves as passionate and simple as they. In any case, since fairies show an obstinacy in learning our ways, we had best be aware of theirs.

Those Who Have Been Spirited Away By Fairies

Young women remarkable for beauty, young men and handsome children are most likely to be spirited away by the fairies. Some men and women wander from the villages to the lonely places and never return; but most are stricken by the fairy blast so that a semblance of themselves seems to sicken and die while their true selves disport on the evergreen lands of faery. Children taken are generally replaced by scrawny, irritable fairy rejects. Some people believe that no one ever 'dies all out'; although visible signs of death are present, apparently all dead humans, they claim, have in actuality been fairy struck. This view corresponds with the notion that fairyland is a Purgatory or Limbo. Furthermore, mortals who had been there reported the dead to be among the *sidhe*. But although fairyland and the land of the dead are on intimate terms (the dead having a propensity for the light-hearted pleasures of the good people and hence frequently found in their company, although fairies are never found in the substanceless world), the two worlds and their inhabitants are distinct.

Fairies delight above all in youth and beauty, hence they gather many of our mortal flowers to adorn their world. Mortal women marry fairy chiefs, men fairy queens. The stolen children grow into fine warriors. In the days of the heroes fairies abducted only queens and kings; but since the royal breed died out, they have learned to be content with more common folk. In those days, too, immortal youth was conferred on all mortals spirited away, but the fairies have rather sparingly bestowed such gifts in the last few centuries. Few mortals now remain beautiful or live forever in fairyland. Most return after seven years, their beauty drained by the intense contact with the *sidhe*. The aged who lived long in fairyland ultimately return home by assuming the forms of dying mortals. Thus, they gently fade and die amongst their own kind.

Those who return and live, return with great gifts. They become famous poets, musicians and fairy doctors. But those who visit fairyland are never quite the same. They are strange and silent, with a wild look in their eyes, and are given to wandering the hills alone in search of the 'gentle' fairy places. One woman was carried off to attend a fairy lady sick on a golden bed; her nursing done, she was granted what she most desired—luck in fishing, learning and gambling for her sons and their descendants. Most are granted gifts, but they do not come out of fairyland unharmed, for some have speech impediments and some have worn away their toes with dancing. Once home, their desire is always for fairyland. Some become 'silly', losing their wits from excess of desire; they soon die in the loneliness of the hills.

There are many methods employed to bring someone back from the fairy places, but the most popular formula is to gather the leaves of the lusmore or foxglove and concoct a tea. If the spirited mortal is only a little touched, she or he will return after a few sips of tea. If she is altogether caught up with fairies, she will refuse the drink and never return. But whoever would administer the tea must first find entry into fairyland. And once there, he must have some charm to ward off the powerful desire to remain.

Fairy Intimates

A number of mortals are on quite intimate terms with the *sidhe*. Frank Martin had been especially baptised against the good people so that he was immune to their harm. A priest had said a proper prayer over him, thus freeing him to mingle with the *sidhe*, to join in their sports and yet come out unscathed by immortal blows. Shawn-Mor often travelled with the good people, carrying their heavy sacks. In exchange they gave him the power to triumph over his enemies; he could handle a dozen at a time. He grew wise with fairy-lore, but with wisdom came conceit, for he soon considered himself as clever as any fairy. The fairies soon set him straight by sending him to the moon on the back of an eagle and leaving him dangling there in space from the end of a pole.

The fairy power can always turn. For if one traffics with powers greater than one's own, one may receive either great blessings or great blows. A gentleman once gave a peasant a florin to buy whiskey; no matter how many times he spent it, the florin reappeared in his pocket. But another was not so lucky. He lived in a house near a fairy fort and whenever he wanted money he would find it on his table. But after this had been going on some time his son died, convincing the man that the death was caused by the back of the hand that gave.

Barney Noonan had a great deal of regard for the good people. Whenever he passed a rath he would slip off his cap, pull the pipe from his mouth and say politely, 'God save ye, ladies and gentlemen'. One wet day they thanked him for his attention by saving his hay from the rain and putting it safely in the barn. Quite joyful over this event, Barney, in a bit too boisterous a manner, demanded the fairies give him a drink to celebrate his good fortune. They were offended by his incivility and took the hay out again to be spoiled by the rain.

Diarmuid Bawn had a bad night but a good reward. The fairies changed him into a horse to help fight another fairy faction. Against the enemy he rode hard for them all night until his faction won. The good people then cordially thanked him for any inconvenience and gave him a tobacco supply to last the rest of his life.

Many a man crossing the lonesome places at night has seen the fairies hurling. The fairies know of his presence, but let him watch, for they like to show off their skill. Most men cannot help but give a cheer at a point well scored. But although fairies do not mind adulation they resent vocal intrusion; and so the shouting men find their heads splitting and senses dazed as they wearily pick themselves off the dewy ground in the morning.

Fairies never have casual relationships with mortals; and men and women should consider carefully whether they want to make the fairies' intimate acquaintance. Once a minister looked too deeply into fairy secrets. He fainted one day while walking on a fairy knoll a little way from his house and died, or so it seemed, immediately thereafter.

The Union of Mortals and Fairies

When a fairy woman falls in love with a mortal, he holds all power over her until he succumbs to her charms. Once he loves, he offers body and soul to her to use as she wills. She consumes him; he joyfully submits. So it is, in more recent times, that a mortal, surrendering to his passion, dies of it. But in the days of the heroes, men and women were equal to fairy love; and since they were granted immortality they still must be celebrating their love to this day. Oisín was a vigorous lover of a fairy woman for three hundred years until he returned to the mortal realm and died. The great warrior Connla still enjoys his fairy lover.

It is small wonder that fairies no longer raid the mortal realm for husbands and brides. Few, if any, of us could endure the strength of their embrace. Yet some still do; and the children of such a union, half-mortal, half-divine, have a passionate nature, given alternately to moody and vengeful fits and long periods of seeming indolence which erupt abruptly into violent emotions. Mortals find these halflings difficult to live with; and they themselves prefer solitude to human contact. Always dissatisfied they wander the hill and converse with unseen spiritual beings.

Perhaps their fretfulness is due to an immortal spirit's struggle against its entrapment within a corruptible body,

37

for, regrettably, they inherit one parent's mortality. Their divine nature makes them impatient with their human limits and hence wild and angry. Perhaps they purposely destroy their bodies so that their souls will the sooner re-enter the fairy kingdom. Surely they are not made for this world, but are only passing time amongst us until they can return to fairyland.

Such contrary beings relinquish human complacency and comfort and are fitful at their work, sometimes absorbed thoroughly in herding or fishing or housekeeping, often indifferent to all but the magic of the hills. Fairy music is in their blood, fairy song upon their lips; without having studied the art or memorised a line they know all the music of the *sidhe* and sing it effortlessly. Their bodies are as beautiful as their songs for all inherit the perfect features and well-proportioned forms of fairyland's creatures. Their eyes are always fiery, their limbs dove-white, taut and desirable. Like hybrid flowers, they are brilliant in colour, bold in form, painfully intense and short-lived.

Fairy Sight and Glamour

Fairies most often appear to the poor and innocent, for they, trusting to their senses, are least likely to be prejudiced about what ought or ought not to exist. Besides, the poor and innocent, having more leisure, consequently have more opportunity to encounter some of the world's less tangible forces. Unless under dire necessity, fairies never hurry down city streets, but they may occasionally be caught idling in city parks. On the whole they prefer the simpler country life, and an unencumbered ramble over fields and hills, so that a poor farmer is more likely to see the good people than his poor, but slightly more sophisticated factory cousin.

The *sidhe*, being most particular about those to whom they appear, disdain traffic with the worldly: a beast sometimes sees more (witness Balaam's ass) than a man, but a man with a gold fob and an air of importance will never see more than a beast; and some fairy women can never be seen by mortal men at all, no matter how innocent or poor they are. Prim moral sticklers declare that only those living in mortal sin can see fairy things; but, of course, they attempt to make a virtue of their blindness. Other christians, craving more frequent intercourse between mortals and fairies, attribute the cause of fairy invisibility to Adam's sin: when humankind fell from grace it also lost easy access to the fairy kingdom.

If one lacks sufficient poverty or innocence, the possession of a four-leafed shamrock adequately compensates; for whoever owns such a clover will see the fairies in full regalia. If shamrocks are scarce, the following procedure is recommended: take a green rush, twist it into a ring and then look through it with one eye. If the fairies are present (and if it is spring or summer they most likely are), you will certainly see them, but you will never have sight in that eye again. Whoever finds a four-leafed shamrock receives the gift of fairy sight; but whoever twists rushes intrudes himself into another's world and must suffer the vengeful consequences. Some visitors to fairyland have purposefully dipped their fingers in the box hung outside the door of the fairy fort, and some have touched the ointment with which the fairies anoint stolen children, and then, unwittingly, touched their eyes. When they left the immortal realm, they took with them the stolen gift of fairy sight. But a fairy soon finds out and smites the eyes without pain, as with a puff of wind, thus depriving them of both the natural and acquired sight. Fortunately, mortals manage to anoint just one eye.

The fairies choose who may see them; even fortuitous four-leafed shamrocks have a habit of lying only in the path of certain people. But as well as granting and withdrawing sight, the fairies also befuddle it. From across the field a farmer might see his house afire, only to find it upright and intact when he runs near to save it. Such is the fairy glamour, or enchantment, which makes mortals see what is not so. Once a whole town witnessed with amazement a cock hauling a huge beam in his beak, while a man with a four-leafed shamrock in his pocket knew that the beam was only a glamourised straw. However, fairies glamourise the world not only for amusement but to take from it what they will by means of darts and blasts without us mortals being the wiser.

Fairy Darts and Blasts

Fairies can make a man live forever or the crops fail over-night. And fairy destruction is as devastating as fairy temper is quick. When angered, fairies hurl at the offender dartlike objects so subtle that they pierce the vitals without breaking the skin. Wherever the darts strike humans or their cattle, a tumour erupts. When fairies are annoyed but not in deadly earnest, they aim at the fingers which become puffy, red and inflamed at the joints. When more severely aggravated, fairies hurl darls with such force that the victim is paralysed and can only, if ever, be cured by a fairy doctor.

Since fairy wrath is subject to instant inflammation, the good people often lack, at the necessary moment, an ample dart supply. But vengeance is inexorable and full of invention. A girl who had accidently interrupted a fairy feast could not walk for several weeks until a fairy doctor removed a tiny tea pot from her thigh. A man who had toyed at night with a skull awoke with a withered leg the next morning. Although he never saw the agent nor felt a smart, he knew for certain he was struck by the fairies for his disrespect. And he was a lucky man, for fairy vengeance is not always so lenient.

Not for revenge alone do fairies attack the mortal realm, nor are they always satisfied with a withered limb. When

40

fairies desire mortals, beasts or crops for their own use, they taken them by what is known as the fairy blast. By means of darts or by projections of their will, fairies blast mortals so that they fall into a deathlike trance while body and soul are translated to fairyland. A healthy man might overnight seemingly become a corpse, but in reality flesh and spirit thrive in a nearby fairy palace. Many a beautiful woman or nursing mother who suddenly seemed to sicken and die, was serving time with the *sidhe*. Sometimes the good people leave a shadowy semblance, sometimes a log of wood fashioned in the woman's form on her deathbed. Many mourners unknowingly grieve over a soulless, substitute form. And how many graves contain no human bones at all, but rotting, mouldy logs?

The fairies usually compensate for the harm they do to mortals. If a wife is blasted, the remaining family prospers. Some consider it lucky to have a fairy-stricken child in the house. Yet one wonders if a lace tablecloth or an abundance of butter compensates adequately for the loss of a child. At least, with the turning of luck, the mother will know that her child is not dead but alive, fingering the golden apples of fairyland.

Fairies will blast a mortal when they desire a lover or nurse, a cow when they need milk for the abducted children and the crops when their larder needs replenishing. To a mortal a new potato might look black and taste like ash, but to a fairy it is hot and buttered and stacked on the table. When the fairies lived above ground they had an easy tillage; but once they moved underground they gave up the work and allowed humans to labour for them.

Some suspect that fairies affect our world not only directly by blasts and touches but by means of certain natural phenomena. Some say the wind is a fairy agent for it too can wither a man. And this may be so; for like the fairies, the wind has power to revive.

A fairy enchanted grass called 'hungry grass' causes anyone who walks upon it suddenly to grow weak with hunger. This happens most often when the traveller is far from home and unsure of the terrain. Luckily the debility caused by this grass is never fatal and usually can be cured by eating a bit of oaten cake.

Some mortals are considered fairy agents for they can 'overlook' or place the evil eye upon their neighbours and their goods, thereby gaining power over them. But these people serve darker forces than the good folk.

Whoever would forego the delights of fairyland should keep well indoors in the month of May, for the fairies are the very fiends for blasting then. And whoever fears the touch of the fool who spirits away mortal wits, should keep indoors as well in the month of June.

When the fairies blast they take all. When they touch or stroke or glance they usually leave a residue on earth. A man who suddenly carries a hump or a cane has suffered from the fairy touch. Often the stroke carries off just the human's soul, leaving the person silly and insensible to external things. Perhaps all those who enter fairyland and return leave some of their soul behind, so that the mortal realm never completely satisfies them. Perhaps the fairy touch is the inevitable curse of mortals whenever our world and faery meet.

Fairy Aids and Preventions

Most mortals would prefer to lock the invisible door between mortal and fairy lands, for the thousands of years of traffic have not always been conducive either to our welfare or to our self-esteem. Since the immortal ones frequently fail to attend to our mortal limitations, it is advisable to have some means of protecting our more delicate bodies and possessions.

Fire is the greatest preventative against magic, fairy or

otherwise, for it is the most heavenly of earthly creations, and man alone of all earth's creatures has the ability to direct it to his will. A ring of fire around the cattle or the baby's cradle or a fire lit under the churn keeps fairy power at bay. In fact, fire is so powerful that the mere smoke of it is enough to check any fairy or phantom. If an island vanishes each time you approach, shoot a flaming arrow at it and it will remain stationary and visible.

Holy water also provides excellent results. A few sprinkles in the usual spots—cradle, churn, cow barn and front door—always do the trick. Prayer, too, is highly efficacious. A 'God bless you' always saves a desired mortal from abduction by the *sidhe*; whenever the fairies travel abroad in the whirlwind, a mortal must cease to speak, cross himself, hold his breath, turn his head aside and recite a short prayer quickly to himself, and the fairy horde will pass him by. If he thrusts his thumb between the fore and middle finger to make the sign of the cross and recites a prayer while passing a fairy location, he is safe from harm. Some say that fairies fear the name of God and consequently their powers wither in the presence of His; but it is more the case that the extraordinary powers respect one another and are careful not to trespass on each other's domain.

Delicate though they are, primroses have great power; scattered before the door or tied to the cows' tails, they guard the house and the cattle from all spirits, especially if they have been freshly picked before sunrise. Mountain ash is an excellent safeguard against magic as are garlands made of marsh marigolds. A four-leafed shamrock is best of all, for the fairies honour it and bedeviled spirits flee from it in horror.

A black-handled knife is a must for escaping from a fairy fort; a pinch of salt will prevent fairy food from affecting mortal wits so that they forget their homelands. The best way to harness a ghost is to place a plough chain around him, for he cannot withstand the power of the blessed

43

instrument. The horse shoe will do as well. Never start a job or a journey or hold a wedding on a Friday for all your endeavours will go awry. If you are prepared to follow all these procedures, you will never be molested by the fairy powers—indeed, the amount of cleverness needed to avoid them will be enough to repulse any of the so-called supernatural beings.

How to Provoke a Fairy

There are certain things fairies will not abide, and they regulate their lands so as to eliminate offensive occurences. All would be well if fairy and mortal lands did not overlap. But they do and fairies maintain their standards with us as well as among themselves. Therefore, in the interest of health and self-preservation, mortals should be informed (the better to be on their guard) as to what provokes the good people.

Dirt offends them. A dirty kitchen stacked with unwashed dishes, a bucket of water fouled by human feet and left standing or a maiden with unkempt hair and filthy fingernails incites their immortal anger. In fact, an untidy mortal forfeits his fate to the fairy powers.

A woman angered the *siahe* because she had thrown a bucket of dirty water at them as they passed invisibly by her door. Of course she would have avoided such an offence if she had seen them, but the good people never attend to such legalisms, no matter how sound the reasoning. If an action offends them, they pay little attention to the cause.

No tree nor rock nor stone should be removed from a fairy rath, for all who tamper with such fairy things invariably die within three days. No one should be so careless as to fall asleep beneath the walls of a fairy fort, for many a mortal limb withered in that sleep, and many a mortal was struck dead altogether. Never build on their paths nor block up their rivers for the fairies travel at furious speeds and an ill-placed house or dam dampens their spirits. Never snigger at a fairy king or queen nor make so bold as to deny either the *sidhe* or their powers.

No mortal should sing or whistle 'The Pretty Girl Milking Her Cow' near a fairy rath for the fairies jealously guard that and all their tunes. When fairies hear their songs on profane mortal lips they are as aesthetically offended as we would be to hear the holy Mass played on a thin tin whistle. In fact, bad taste irritates the fairies as much as discourtesy.

Before a mortal eats of meat he should inquire into the cause of the animal's death; for if the animal did not die naturally but had been stricken by the *sidhe* for their particular purposes, the offending mortal invariably incurs the good people's wrath. Most of all a mortal should never inquire too deeply about the *sidhe* or their world, for those who pry too much into fairy affairs may never live to write books about them.

A mortal who would keep on good terms with the *sidhe* must refrain from all too human vices of untidiness, vulgarity, discourtesy and intrusion. In fact, in order not to provoke the fairies, one must develop and maintain a graceful, aristocratic manner.

Fairy Justice

The family that leaves a sip of wine in the glass and some potatoes on the platter secures the fairies' good grace. The good people appreciate such marks of deference and in turn ensure that the roof never leaks, the hens always lay and the children have straight limbs and strong teeth. They are an upright and honest folk, repaying a good deed with one better. But while their blessings are ample, their vengeance is deadly and sure. A man once aided a wizened old fairy to steal a fairy woman, but was so love-smitten that he robbed her for himself. Like lightening the fairy blighted his fields, and his forty head of cattle shrivelled to nought with the blast. To be sure no help from Heaven came to the man who broke the back of the fairy piper. Not a potato stalk stood upright with all the hail pommelling the land for miles around. And woe to the family that refuses a fairy admittance, for the curse will never be lifted until the last of the family is laid in the grave.

Fairies speedily avenge any injustice, not only that done to their own. They have stolen a child from its mother when she failed to wash and pray for it. They have beaten a man until he was nothing but a bruise because he daily indulged in beating his wife.

The fairies are an open-handed but fastidious race who regard it as their particular office to punish the niggardly and chastise the untidy. Being innocent creatures they are stern upholders of virtue and have little traffic with mercy.

Cows

Cows, like beautiful women, are particularly sensitive to the fairy powers; therefore a good deal of prevention is needed to keep them from fairy abduction. They graze often about fairy raths (the grass is literally greener there for the good people have a way with growing things) and roam into secluded places where men hardly venture and hence where fairies sport. Since fairies have a penchant for cows' milk (with what else would they feed the abducted children?), they often induce a cow to leave her accustomed pasture, while they leave a substitute form behind to convince the mortal master of the cow's illness and consequent death.

A cow name Cooby was a great visitor to the fairy forts, until her master tethered her and kept her home. She then languished for want of fairy grass; her milk failed her and she died. Her owner then skinned and ate her, or so he thought, but in fact he consumed nothing but an old stray horse with the glamour upon her. A stray horse could easily be dispensed with, but the fairies needed Cooby to feed the abducted, nurseless children. Later the man saw his cow grazing again in the fort and, overcoming his fears, he quickly reclaimed her. So tenaciously did he argue that in respect the good people returned his cow, which had served her purpose, and favoured him further with great wealth.

Fairies are not generally inclined to return what they have taken, nor do they (with their inadequate comprehension of things past) respect the claim of prior ownership. It is better strategy to keep what one has than to gamble on its return. Fairies always hanker after cows and cow products, but on the eve of May their desire grows maniacal. On all days, but especially May eve, a mortal must be skilled in all the fairy preventive arts of fire, holy water, primroses, etc., in order to keep the milk in the cow, the butter in the churn and the cow in the field. Having a cow and a calf, John Hanifin wisely gave the cow's milk to a fairy mother for her child. Because of his thoughtfulness, she allowed him to keep the milk of the calf. But when, in her greed, his wife tried to milk the cow, she found it stripped, as was the calf, leaving her nothing for her effort. Therefore it is advisable to share one's milk with the fairies, for if they are not given half they are inclined to take the whole.

Human Changelings

Any mortal spirited away to fairyland and replaced by a fairy semblance is a changeling. A jovial good-humoured buck who overnight appears to become a meagre, disagreeable creature with pinched features, a harsh voice and a craving appetite actually lives hale and hearty in fairyland. Even a cow that has been taken and replaced by a nag in cow's form is a changeling. But the term most often applies to children, baptised or not, abducted by the good people who leave wizened creatures (fairy changelings) as substitutes. The mother readily notes the difference between the sweet darling who is gone and the crotchety sniveller who grabs with gnarled nails at her breast. Curiously, only male infants are taken; fairies wait until the girls babies blossom into womanhood and then select the most beautiful.

Some claim that fairies have power only over unbaptised babes; but, although this is generally the case, they also exercise control over children whose mothers have forgotten to say prayers and to sprinkle appropriate amounts of holy water over them. Fairies contentedly share human spoils with christianity: what one does not want, the other might have.

It is generally the mother's own fault if her child is changed, for it is her duty to baptise, bless and wash it. Fairies loathe negligence and justly punish the negligent mother with the loss of her child. A neighbour, too, who enviously regards a child makes it thereby susceptible to fairy powers. There are, of course, many precautions one can take. McAlister claims that if a mother made the sign of the cross on the infant's face with ashes, bit off the fingernails until the child was nine weeks old, held a burning candle in front of its eyes as often as possible, gave it a daily mixture of sugar, salt and oil and tied a four-leafed shamrock round its neck, the fairies surely would pass it up for an easier mark. But proper care, a light constantly burning, a bit of holy water, a prayer, a cross over the door, all singly or combined, usually suffice, making elaborate preventive measures excessive.

In the case of changelings, an ounce of prevention outweighs a pound of cure, for the most acclaimed method of reclaiming one's child is to set the fairy replacement on a red-hot shovel and either throw it on a dungheap or into a chimney fire. The fairy changeling will leap howling back to fairyland, while his human counterpart will be found innocently asleep at home in the cradle. But one must be assured of the change, for a case has been reported of a man who roasted his child to death, believing it was a fairy.

If one balks at the red-hot shovel method, it is advisable to leave the fairy changeling alone and assail the fairy fort where the real child is hidden. Threatening to burn down a fairy fort is an effective method if the fairies believe you can make good your threat. Another more tried method is to tie a skein of black flax thread around the left hand, with a black-handled knife well gripped in the right. The thread keeps one in contact with the mortal realm, while the power of the black-handled knife thwarts opposing fairy forces. The thread should be tied to a briar outside the door of the fairy fort, and as one enters the thread should unwind until one has reached the kitchen, where the child will inevitably be found. Take the child up and if it has not yet drunk three times of enchanted breast milk, it can be brought safely home.

Beautiful Women and Nursing Mothers

Fairies claim all beautiful things (including humans) as their own and they always need fine, strong women to nurse the stolen young. Therefore, beautiful women and nursing mothers frequently take up residence in fairyland.

Many a high-spirited girl climbed the mountains never to return; many a colleen, gazing down into a lake, sang so soulfully of her heart's desire that she spent the next seven years looking upward and singing from a sea palace below. The fairies gather beauty as a young girl wild flowers; and they as willingly discard them once the bloom is gone. The immortal ones have no compassion for the messy decay and death of the human race. They require lovely women in their prime; some just for an evening (their forms seemingly

49

lying abed) to dance with the wild king Fionvarra; some for the allotted seven years to wed and dance each night with fairy chiefs in impassioned embraces.

The intensity of fairy life ravishes them, and they return home to the mortal realm as shrivelled, old hags. Some return home with no toes, having danced them away. Yet despite their deformities their eyes flame and their voices quiver with longing. Although mortals respect them as grand fairy doctors, they shrug off the honours; when humans offer companionship they head for the quiet places where fairies are reputed to be.

Humans are made of strange yearning stuff; they always desire what has passed or what will never be. Therefore the fairies, secure in eternity and awake to the present, have difficulty understanding their mortal brethren. Like mortals they are ravished by desire; but it never withers them. Rather, it tunes them finely like a well-used lyre which plays sweeter the more it is stroked. When a mortal woman desires so that her very marrow aches, she is most like the fairies, and they embrace her as kin in Tír-na-n-Óg. A young girl once died of desire for fairy music. To honour her passion the fairies caused delicate roses to grow on her grave. Most women die when seized with longing for fairy things; but a few, a very rare few, overcome death by desire, and thus remain young and eternal among the *sidhe*.

Fairy interest in nursing mothers is of a much more practical nature; consequently their term of residence is of shorter duration. Fairies abduct them to nurse stolen, mortal children and sometimes fairy children whose mothers are sickly after the birth. At night they return home to feed their own, thus giving a husband an opportunity to reclaim his wife. After sunset the stolen woman appears about the house, sometimes as a venomous snake, sometimes as a wrinkled hag in a pall; but the devoted husband braces himself, saying never a word, and gives her something to eat so that she may refuse the fatal fairy food. Eventually she will regain her own form to give suck to the child. If she falls asleep on the third night, all is well. The man quickly stretches a red string across the threshold to prevent the fairies' entry; then, in the name of God, he sprinkles her with holy water. She will then reassume her true form and remain at home as blithe as ever.

There are many methods for reclaiming a stolen woman. Some are quite complicated since beautiful women, unlike nursing mothers, are not allowed to return home. One must, therefore, go to the fairies. Since it is nearly impossible to catch the fairies napping at home, a husband or lover had best discover them when they travel abroad. Sometimes it takes months of searching hills and graveyards until they are found. But if he is intent in his pursuit, he carries a black-hafted knife and waits for the troop to ride out at night. Since fairy troops travel screened by whirlwind and mist, it is nearly impossible to distinguish one rider from another, yet the determined man always manages to do so. At the first rider that passes he stabs hard and once only, for a second thrust would undo the harm. The mist about the troop vanishes at once; the woman then clearly appears. By force he pulls her from her horse, drawing her close to him in a ring made of holy water, which the fairies dare not transgress. Within the ring he anoints her with chosen herbs gathered near the fairy fort. Protected by the herbs she can safely return home. But if the man slips up on any of these steps, he will lose his woman forever.

Since fairies generally leave a replacement for those women (especially nursing mothers) they abduct on a temporary basis, a man may be fortunate enough to have an image substituted for the true wife. If this is the case, his task is simple. While the false form sleeps, he unfastens her girdle and tosses it into the fire, making sure to bury the pin that bound it under the earth. The false form will vanish; the true return; and the man need never concern himself with black-hafted knives and fairy riders. As long as the pin lies safely buried, the flesh-and-blood woman can live contentedly at home with her man.

Women with husbands most often return. Not only are husbands most skilled in procuring their escape, but married women themselves do not acclimatise properly to fairyland. They persist in their previous attachments. Unmarried girls, however, need think only of themselves, and being purer in intent, adjust more easily to fairy custom.

Musicians

Although fairies jealously guard their own songs, they trespass our lands to listen to good mortal-made music. Suspect the presence of the good people at weddings, wakes and céilí mórs; for they dance upon a neighbouring hill or, invisble, mingle among the guests. Sometimes they dally under the eaves, listening to the piper or concertinist within.

Maurice, king of the Munster pipers, had such an excellent time that he set to dancing all mortals on land and all fish in the sea, until a beautiful merrow queen, yielding to her desire and swaying voluptuously on the waves, tenderly offered herself to him and a submarine kingship. What could he do but accept? And now the sea muffles the sound of his pipe from mortal ears.

One night the champion fiddler of all north Kerry hobbled over a hill, fiddle in hand and withered leg dragging behind, on his way home from a wedding. As he passed by a fairy rath the good people hailed him and requested a tune. Since the *sidhe*'s reputation discourages all discourtesy, the man did not refuse, but took up his fiddle, though he was weary with sleep, and played the sweetest music until dawn without missing a note. The next morning he swaggered home on two sound legs. But the lame man who scratched them a tune like the screeching of cats could not step at all for both his legs became as weak as milk.

Similarly a certain hunchback lost his burden having improved a tiresome fairy tune, while a second man earned two hunches for his musical pretence.

Fairies favour all the beautiful and talented in our land, but upon musicians they bestow their greatest honours. To them they grant prosperity and success in love. But usually the reward for fine music is abduction. A young girl singing by a lake sang for the next seven years in an underwater fairy palace. Since fairies cannot always spend their time hanging about the eaves of our houses or waylaying fiddlers on their way home from a dance, they steal our finest musicians to provide exclusive and continuous performances in fairyland.

Fairy Doctors

Fairy doctors never spend years at the university learning the medical arts, but receive the knowledge as a direct gift from the fairies. A woman once carried a fine fairy lady across the river on her back to prevent her sullying her dress; the next morning she knew the virtue of all plants and herbs and immediately started a practice. The good people once gave Lee a medical book with instructions not to open it for seven years. But as he was a kind-hearted soul, he opened it after three years to cure an ailing cousin. Only three years of knowledge was legible in that great leather book, all the rest blackened and flaked off like charred wood. Yet, even with his four-year lack, he knew enough to be more effective than ten ordinary doctors.

Most fairy doctors are women because they are, at least in Ireland, more susceptible than men to the fairy influence. Perhaps it is because they more willingly submit to events, rather than feel compelled to capture and control all things with their wills. In any case, most fairy doctors are women and many were once beautiful women stolen from their homes to wed or pleasure fairy men. After seven years, when they return home, grey and passion-spent, they bring with them the wisdom of curing as a compensation for their premature withering. Having wed the male fairies, they decline to mate with their own, and hence remain childless and self-dependent.

Maurice Griffen received the fairy gift in a most curious manner. His cow ate a white bit of foam that floated down from the skies and landed on the grass in front of her. She was then milked of four extraordinary foamy pitchers of which Maurice had the great good fortune to drink three, thus gaining knowledge of herbal cures. He was a married man who passed the art on to his wife when he died, for that is the way with fairy doctors—they are required to choose a successor but never impart their knowledge until they know that death awaits them. But generally if a doctor is not a woman, he is an unmarried man, for a bachelor more likely than a man with a wife roams the fields at night.

There is also a method of curing recommended for the amateur who has never had much dealing with the fairies. If she or he would go out at night and kill and dress a sheep, making sure to pick the right shoulder bone as clean as possible, and then sleep with it under the pillow, she would know the cure for any disease, since the bone will talk professionally to her while she sleeps.

Fairy doctors cure by means of charms and incantations; they never pierce the skin for they respect the fairies' distaste for blood. Fairy-doctoring is a much less messy affair than our modern-day methods and hence greatly to be preferred. By measuring a man with an ordinary rule, they know his entire medical history. And with their intuitive knowledge, they competently treat most complaints. Naturally they are the only mortals qualified to cure the fairy blast.

Biddy Early was one of the best, if what Lady Gregory tells us be true, for she could cure all things save the stroke of the fool. Like all of her ilk, she never took a shilling in payment for her charms because money depreciates, among other things, the healing effect. Fairy arts are a gift not to be bartered. But fairy doctors accept most donations of bread and beer.

Since great dangers accompany fairy-doctoring, many a practitioner has retired early from the trade. Although faires have given certain mortals power to countermand their own deeds, they perversely dislike it when those mortals exercise that power. Oftentimes the fairies take offence when a doctor cures a mortal they have blasted and desired for their own. In revenge they lead the healer out into a field and thrash her so lustily that she herself is most in need of healing charms. By curing others fairy doctors often endanger their own and their relations' lives; and few nowadays are humanitarian enough to pursue for long a self-detrimental occupation. There is always a compensation for occult wisdom and those who traffic with powers greater than themselves can as easily be obliterated as favoured. Balancing between two worlds is, at best, a dubious occupation.

Priests have always possessed the healing power but are not willing hands at it these days. In Ireland's days of glory they risked their own health for that of their parish; but with the years and the good living, they do not, even in sore times, admit to the power or to the name of those who gave it.

III

THE SOLITARY FAIRIES

The Solitary Fairies

The solitary fairies abide by themselves, either because they disdain the eternal gaiety of their trooping comrades or because a fatal attraction draws them away from their own to mortal lands. Sometimes they lavish great gifts upon us mortals, but the consequences of accepting them are often dire. Contact with a solitary one is often disruptive if not fatal to a mortal's life. Many solitary fairies have been falsely accused of being in league with the devil; many are, however, on intimate terms with Death.

The leprechaun guards the fairy treasure, and hence is a solitary hoarder, whose personality disgruntles the trooping sort. The lianhan shee lusts for mortals; female merrows desire human husbands. The banshee and dullahan know death and hence are acquainted with mortality. Ghosts, although the do not originate in fairyland, visit that realm and ours. The pooka and far darrig delight in our discomfort; changelings come to live and die frequently in our lands. Fairy animals often stray in our grasslands; and assorted human-like creatures wander about our world, bringing luck or harm.

These fairies are not indifferent to our mortal world, and therefore we have most contact with them. Their personalities differing radically from those of the blithe trooping fairies, the solitary fairies, avoiding their brethren, gravitate towards the sober, trouble-filled mortal world.

Leprechauns and Cluricauns

The leprechaun is a solitary creature avoiding contact not only with mortals but with other leprechauns, and, indeed, with the entire fairy tribe. He cannot endure their fickle frivolity nor they his dour manner. While trooping fairies delight in variegated experience, he pours all the passion of his concentrated soul into the careful making of shoes. A leprechaun will always be found with a shoe in one hand and a hammer in the other.

All leprechauns are ugly, stunted creatures, no taller than boys of ten or twelve, but broad and bulky, with faces like dried apples. But their eyes are always mischievously alight, and their bodies, despite their stubbiness, lithe. Leprechauns disappear behind trees faster than the mortal eye can follow.

And despite their possession of all the earth's treasure, they never sport clothes more elegant than drab, usually grey-coloured coats, sturdy leather pocket-studded aprons and, for a bit of colour, dusty-red cocked hats.

Leprechauns are a querulous, sottish and foul-mouthed breed—the bane of the fairer fairylanders. They smoke ill-smelling stumps of pipes called dudeens and guzzle intemperate draughts of beer from ever handy jugs. But the fairy gentry endure them because they provide the much needed service of cobblery. A few nights of intensive fairy dancing wear even the sturdiest of shoes; and so the leprechauns must ply their trade assiduously to meet the fairy demand. Luckily, drinking never unsteadies the hand holding the hammer.

Leprechauns guard the fairies' treasure as well as shoe their feet. Not only must they prevent the theft of treasure by mortals, but they must avert its waste by their profligate trooping brethren. Trooping fairies do not understand the value of a ruby nor care to store for the future. They are lavish when they have, indifferent when they have not.

Without the leprechauns as bankers, the fairies would centuries ago have squandered their fortune within and without their borders. Since treasure belongs to all fairies, any fairy can spend, much to the leprechauns' chagrin, what he wills. And so although leprechauns grumble, they begrudgingly give what is asked; for, in truth, leprechauns live in awe of their fine-featured relatives.

Unlike the trooping fairies, the solitary fairies have a memory for the past. The trooping *sidhe* cannot keep abreast of short-lived mortal affairs; the solitary fairies never forget, but limit their interests. Whereas the banshees recall great mortal deeds, leprechauns (alone of the *sidhe*) remember when the marauding Danes landed in Ireland and where they hid their treasure. This memorable virtue, coupled with a remembrance of subsequent burials, gives leprechauns the decided advantage in treasure-guarding.

Although leprechauns bury their treasure well to keep it from profligate fairy and greedy mortal hands, rainbows frustrate their efforts by rudely settling themselves over particular gold hordes. By its presence a rainbow alerts mortals to a treasure's whereabouts, thereby causing the guardian-leprechaun incalculable anxiety. No matter how fast the little creature moves his pot, he never eludes the adherent rainbow. Luckily he usually manages to elude the grasp of the pursuant mortal, always baffled at the rainbow's inaccessibility.

If a mortal catches a leprechaun (a possible task due to his absorption in treasure-counting and his frequent over-indulgence in drink), he must closely hold the little fellow, fixing an eye on him, and sternly demand his treasure. The leprechaun never refuses. But only a rare man actually recovers the horde. Invariably the leprechaun manages to turn the man's head—perhaps with a tale of his favourite horse's fall into the sinking bog—and, like a greased pig, slips from the tight grip. Once a man forced a leprechaun to disclose a treasure buried beneath a tree. Tying a red scarf around the tree to mark it, the man then dashed home for a spade, having elicited from the leprechaun an oath to touch neither scarf nor treasure. And neither did he. But when the man returned, every tree in the wood sported a red scarf.

Since mortals and fairies either avoid them or approach them to exact their gold, leprechauns have become accustomed to trust only themselves. But kind acts sentimentally affect them and prompt them to respond in a generous manner. Sometimes in a moment of alcoholic geniality a leprechaun offers a mortal not only a drink but some of his treasure, or a shilling contained in a leather purse having the property of perpetual replenishment. An impoverished nobleman who had given a wee fellow a lift on his horse found his dilapidated castle the next day stacked to its leaky ceiling with gold coins. Once a leprechaun with a sentimental streak gave his treasure to a man claiming part-leprechaun blood. And on an extraordinarily generous occasion one gave a golden bridle which, whenever shaken, produced a strong yellow steed attached to it.

Female leprechauns do not exist; and since female fairies and mortals find the males physically repulsive, leprechaun-reproduction is doubtful. Leprechauns themselves are reticent about their births as they are secretive about most things. Perhaps they were the defective children of beautiful fairy parents who ejected them from the fairy troop because of their shape and disposition, but endured their separated existences as long as they cobbled shoes and guarded treasure.

Much debate has arisen as to whether cluricauns are actually leprechauns or degenerate close cousins. Save for a pink tinge about the nose, cluricauns perfectly resemble leprechauns in all their physical construction. But they never sport an apron or carry a hammer or manifest any desire to work. They look and act like week-end gentlemen: silver buckles adorn their shoes, gold laces their caps and pale blue stockings their stocky calves. They unabashedly

59

enter rich men's wine cellars as if they were their own and drain the casks. For amusement they harness sheep and goats and shepherds' dogs, jump the bogs and race them over the fields through the night until the beasts are muddy and beaten with fatigue.

Leprechauns sternly declare these pleasure-seekers to be none of their own. Those believing their word argue that while extravagantly clothed cluricauns tipple the wine glass, self-respecting leprechauns in working dress drink nothing but beer. Yet since cluricauns do act like working men putting on aristocratic airs, many suspect them to be nothing other than leprechauns on a spree, who, in the sobering morning, haughtily deny a perverse double nature. The question remains insoluble because neither reckless drunkards nor creatures with reputations to preserve can be thoroughly trusted.

Far Darrig (Red Man)

The far darrig (or fear dearg) is a near relation to the leprechaun, with similar puckered features and a short stocky body. His face is splotched as yellow as buttermilk clots; he dresses in red from his sugar-loaf hat to his tail-trailing cape to the woollen stockings which cling to his calves. Hence his name—the far darrig or red man. He is reputed not only for his colour (for he sometimes travels invisibly) but for his delight in all varieties of mischief and mockery, especially in gruesome practical joking. He manipulates his voice most wondrously, emitting sounds like the thudding of waves on rocks or the cooing of pigeons; his forte is the dull, hollow laugh of a dead man from within a vast and rain-sodden tomb.

Mortal terror amuses the far darrig. On occasion he invites a mortal to enter a lonely bog hut, whereupon he orders him to make dinner out of a naked hag skewered on a spit. The man invariably faints. When he recovers, he finds himself alone and chilled on the bog with the sound of derisive laughter swelling the air, but coming from no distinguishable source. It is advisable to say *'Ná déan magadh fúm'*— 'do not mock me'—upon encountering a far darrig, lest one be caught fast in some macabre game. Unfortunately, he plans his tricks so cleverly that a mortal is snared long before he realises the need to protest. Preventive measures, at that point, no longer apply.

Ironically, with all his pranks, the far darrig desires not to do harm but to show favour. He is actually a good natured sort, bringing luck to those whom he approves; but he cannot resist a preliminary teasing. A notorious far darrig named Teigue constantly frequented a certain house; the room echoed with his unearthly laughter but he never injured the inhabitants or their guests. Teigue instinctively knew each one's secrets and accomplishments; and he had a particular fondness for music. If any had musical talents which they were too modest to profess, he never politely requested a performance, but methodically terrorised them into admitting their ability and giving a tune.

Whenever Teigue entered the house he cordially greeted the master and requested his usual glass of whiskey. A far darrig likes his comfort, and assumes that mortals are conveniently placed on earth to administer to it. A comfortable hearth in winter, a good shot of poteen and a filled pipe by the sofa are the minimum requirements. And if the house is clean and well-regulated the red man so works his fairy will that equanimity sustains itself and the household prospers.

A certain far darrig entered the house of his choice each evening promptly at eleven o'clock. He expected fire, pipe and whiskey in their respective places and the inhabitants safe in bed. Each night he stuck his hairy little arm through the keyhole, opened the door and made himself at home. Fearing his vengeance (for, if crossed, he was likely to destroy them or their cattle), the family acceded to his eccen-

61

tricities and so became rich and remained healthy. Yet when they moved he refused to go, but awaited the accustomed service from the new tenants. Evidently, red men attach themselves to houses and not families.

Although the far darrig enjoys his comfort, he likes a modicum of adventure. Whenever fairies of foreign parts attack his lands, he quits his solitary comfort, jumps on a well-groomed steed and effectively commands the native fairy forces. If mortals inadvertently cross his path, he saddles and bridles them and converts them into war-horses for the battle's duration. Such happened to Diarmuid Bawn, the piper, who became a lead-charger for the victorious faction and was consequently rewarded with a lifetime supply of tobacco for the midnight service.

Some claim that the red men are humans who return from the dead either because they found Heaven or Hell excessive or the mortal life-style eternally satisfactory. But red men are, in truth, fairy men who, never quite adjusting to manic fairy habits, have always harboured a sentimental affection for the more subdued manners of humankind.

Merrows and Silkies

Fine or bad weather, the male merrow sits on a rock, scanning the sea for cases of brandy loosed from wrecked ships. He is a most amiable fellow with a red nose (some say from an over-indulgence in the above-mentioned liquor) and a bringer of good luck. He wears a cocked hat and is green in body, with green hair and teeth; he has pigs' eyes and scaly legs, arms like fins, and wears no clothes at all. Small wonder it is that the beautiful female merrows seek husbands in mortal lands.

The female merrow is lovely and lithe, with graceful fish tails and fine web-like scales between the fingers. Her gown is as white as the sea foam, trimmed simply with red and purple sea weeds; and her hair, with the salt water upon it, shines like dew struck by morning light. Like the male merrow, she wears a red cocked hat which charmingly suits her alluring face with its mocking eyes. Sometimes a dark mantle clings about her, half-revealing the full curves of her figure.

The female merrow impudently teases men with her beauty. Negligently she lounges, attracting fishermen to her sea rock; but if a curragh approaches too near, she dives into the sea, laughing at the love-enchanted men above. And little joy they get from her, for her presence always ensures a storm. She upsets the waves and brings the rains down from the sky. Ships at sea are cracked like straws. curragh and rafts in the lough capsize. For the female merrow of the sea, the storm and the destruction make for a delightful diversion from her voluptuous indolence.

On the sea she is as wild as she is lovely, but on land she becomes shy and submissive to men. Fishermen who have suffered from the female emigration from Ireland linger by the seaways long after work in hopes that a female merrow might appear. For if a man can but capture her red cap or dark mantle, she will forget her past watery life and quietly accompany him to the altar. Obedient and loving, the merrow makes a most excellent wife. But although mindful of her husband and of her household duties, she never quite adjusts to land-living. A married merrow rarely laughs and never has a jolly, fun-loving temperament. A quiet caring is her greatest emotion.

But if she finds her cap (which the solicitous husband always inadequately hides and never destroys), and sets it on her head, she remembers her carefree life in her sub-marine palace and joyfully abandons her home and her mate for the sea. After years of marriage a merrow dis-covered her mantle in the closet and could not resist the temptation to try it. Immediately she forgot her child crying in the cradle; and regaining the youth and beauty she

63

lost among mortals, she returned to her eternal, reckless splendour.

Gentler creatures are the silkies who are seals by day but men and women at night. Silently they emerge from the sea to shed their skins and disport on the sand. Like the merrows they have webs between their fingers and toes and must obey anyone who secures their oily skins. Silkies, too, make excellent wives; but they, being solitary, quiet creatures by nature, frequently wander from their mortal homes to the sea cliffs to meditate and sing their melancholy songs. When their fishermen-husbands are lost upon the sea, they sing from the cliffs to guide them home.

Banshees and Keening

A wail of exquisite sweetness piercing the night, its notes rising and falling like the waves of the sea, always announces a mortal's death. Such is the awesome keen of the banshee, the solitary woman fairy, mourning and forewarning those of the high Milesian race, those whose names begin with 'Mac' and 'Ó', whose origin dates from the time of the Irish heroes, that death is impending. The banshee loves the old mortal families with a fierce and unearthly caring. Having fused her life's blood with that of the great heroes, she wailed for fear and for encouragement as they rode into battles; and when they died her soul was seared, her sensibilities raw and bleeding. So she wails, sometimes in a caressing bitter-sweet voice, sometimes in a shriek like one struck by a sudden and mortal blow, making tree roots tremble, for those heroes' descendants. For her, the past reverberates in the present; each keen embraces centuries of remembered glory.

When a member of the beloved race is dying, she paces the dark hills about his house. Sharply contrasted against the night's blackness, her white figure emerges with silver-grey hair streaming to the ground and a grey-white cloak of a cobweb texture clinging to her tall thin body, shivering violently from cold and grief. So thin is she that it seems the wind could crack her like a brittle twig. Her face is as pale as a corpse, her eyes red-bloated with centuries of crying. Gaunt as Mary Magdalene and as dedicated, she inspires in those who see her an awe at such intense emotion and a pity, too, for so weak a frame.

White Lady of Sorrow some people name her, and Lady of Death. She is the Woman of Peace and the Spirit of the Air. Her name means woman (ban) fairy (shee). For despite her shrieks and gnashings, she somehow exhibits a divine nature, graced with an insurpassable nobility of manner. Imposing and beautiful upon the hills, she points the way to the dying man's or woman's house, her stance defiant, her bearing dignified by centuries of imperial command. None dare evade her death notice.

Unseen banshees attend the funerals of the beloved dead, but sometimes the keen swells so fierce in their breasts that their lips must give voice. Blending in with the general shrieking and bemoaning of the dead, the keen often goes unnoticed. Some say that banshees sometimes howl with a demonic delight at the coming death-agony of their mortal enemies—of those who defied the family they cherish; and this may be so for they nurture their hatred as well as their love.

Each banshee has her own mortal family; in their great deeds she exults; at their deaths she rips out her hair and claps her hands in despair. Out of love she follows the old race across the ocean to distant lands. Her keen can be heard in America and England, wherever the true Irish have been forced to settle. But they never forget their blood ties; and neither does she. Fairies inhabit all the world's countries; but the banshee keens only among the Irish.

The Lianhan Shee

The lianhan shee is a fairy woman of dreadful power, for she seeks the love and dominion of mortal men. Only one lianhan shee exists and she is more a force than a woman. Yet each fairy woman who loves ('Lianhan Shee' means the love fairy) becomes one with her; and for the mortal man who longs for her she is the one and only. When the lianhan shee appears, nothing else exists. She does not trifle with emotions; all who love her live for her and exult in their desire which frequently destroys them. The more suffering she inflicts the dearer she becomes to them. The more they desire her the more she eludes them, her absence like a fine chain pulling them towards her.

Connla the Bold saw a woman upon a hill who called to him and offered herself and eternal beauty in the Land of the Living. Although all heard her words, no one but he saw her. Desirous he reached towards her, but she threw him an apple to stay his pursuit. For a month he ate of nothing but the ever-sustaining apple; no other food nor drink appealed. No thoughts but of her concerned him. He forgot his people and ignored the words of his friends. And when the woman sent him a crystal boat, he joyfully leaped into it, sailing towards her with never a backward look. Connla was never seen again, but assuredly now, as always, he enjoys his love in the Land of the Heart's Desire.

A fairy woman visited Angus Óg by dream. Each night for a year she played silver music for him on a harp. When he reached towards her she vanished; but when he lay still, she sat by his bedside and lulled him to sleep. At the year's end her visits stopped and Angus grew ill with love-longing. Physicians found no physical ailments; only the presence of his beloved could cure him. Finally, after endless searching, he found her in the shape of a swan; and since he could not live without her, he too became a bird. The music they made as they flew rang so sweetly that all who heard it fell asleep for three days and three nights.

An impatient mistress, the lianhan shee creates such desire in her lovers than they overcome all obstacles to embrace her. She never yields to them in mortal lands, but insists on their meeting in Tír-na-n-Óg, so that men must pass through death to enjoy her. All the great poets and musicians loved her; almost all died young. She rent their hearts and in their blood-agony began song. The more they sang the more their bodies withered; until they sang for her forever.

No one has ever described the lianhan shee. Perhaps each stricken man jealously guards his love and fears the world's knowledge of her. But more likely no mortal can describe her; for ineffable as desire itself, the lianhan shee eludes all attempts to limit her glory. She may select her lovers from our realm, but she never allows her story to remain long on their mortal lips.

Fairy Changelings

When a mother finds a scrawny, ill-tempered, foul-mouthed yellow-faced little man in the cradle, she knows instantly that the fairies have traded her boy for this thing. The dwarfed form and petulant manner convince some that the creature is actually a child, but a clever mother realises that a fairy changeling has entered her home.

Naturally each substitute has a distinctive personality; but ugliness and ill temper are generic changeling traits. Fairies, in their immortal perfection, are aesthetically repulsed by these creatures with their restless, coal-burnt eyes, puckered features and parchment-textured skin; hence they eject them from their lands. And their whines, yowls and screeches so aggravate humans that we, in our less than immortal endurance, immediately attempt to eject them from ours.

Before they live a year in our world, they grow a full mouth of teeth; their hands are like kites' claws, their legs no thicker than chicken bones. Their mischief knows no limit; their eyes are alive with malice for the human race. No matter how much food they devour, they still whine for more, yet remain as runty as ever. After a farmer labours to feed a changeling's gluttonous appetite, little remains for the rest of the family.

A family whose son is abducted may receive as a substitute a sickly fairy child or a log of wood bewitched to look like their own, which soon appears to sicken and die. They bury and mourn it, never realising that their own child plucks the flowers of fairyland. Yet despite their grief and ignorance, they are more fortunate to suffer such a loss than to have a pinched-featured, hairy, ravenous, wild thing pounding the floors and raiding the cupboards.

Placing a set of bagpipes by the cradle is a sure test to discover whether the child is a fairy. No changeling can resist them; their scrawny hands would as soon reach for the pipes as for a mother's teat. Soon the fairy music spills out of the house and into the village, paralysing with joy those within and without. Surely not even Baby Mozart displayed such a skill, let alone a six-month's child.

Brewing egg shells is another fool-proof fairy detecting method. A mother, under a fairy doctor's instructions, boiled egg shells in front of the suspected child. In an old man's voice, the changeling cackled with laughter at the notion of making dinner from shells.

To dispose of changelings masking as mortals, two time-tested methods are recommended: (1) heat a red-hot shovel, shovel the fairy up and cast him onto a dungheap or into a chimney fire and (2) force foxglove tea down his throat and wait until it burns out his entrails. Amazingly, no matter how brutal the punishment of the fairy the original child always returns unscathed.

Some fairy changelings are time-worn fairies; others are

aged humans who long ago were spirited away to fairyland. Their common quality is an unfitness for the beauty and grace of fairyland. Most changelings are time-worn fairies who have retained their immortality but not their beauty. Some, through mishaps, become physically defective and hence rejected. A jobber, for example, once intruded into a fairy fort where he broke the back of a fairy piper. So disabled was the fairy that the *sidhe* disclaimed him as a member and substituted him for a wholesome child in a cradle. The rocking of the cradle jolted his back, making him yowl; and his bagpipe ability made folks suspect his origin. Fairies may never die, but they can be maimed and hence forfeit their rights to fairyland.

Other changelings are humans taken years ago and then sent back to the mortal realm to receive the last rites. Some slanderers assert that when fairies take a cow or a heifer they leave in its place an old person in a beast-semblance. They claim that a man can never know if he is eating his grand-mother when he eats an animal that has had a suspicious death. But these are vicious lies perpetuated by those delighting in the accusation of sin. Old people do return but never in beast form. They never become yowling changelings, discontented with mortal surroundings, but quietly assume the semblance of sickly children. And quietly they pass into death and are properly buried.

The Red-Haired Man, the Dark Man, the Grey Man and the Man of Hunger

In the fairy realm lives a red-haired man who, for no clear reason, has an affinity for the mortal race. He warns a young woman to refuse the wine or leads the spell-drugged young man out of the fairy fort. Whenever someone sneezes at a party, he says the necessary 'God bless you' to prevent abduction. More mortals would have been taken to, and fewer returned from, fairyland without the intervention of this benevolent, red-haired fairy man.

The dark man or the far dorocha, however, is a chief agent in mortal abduction. He exclusively serves the fairy queen: at her command he brings in the tea tray or rides on his black charger to our realm to escort back mortals she desires. A perfect butler, he never betrays emotion nor wastes a movement. Direct from fairyland, back erect, face set and with never a glance about him, he rides until he encounters the desired mortal. Although he never speaks, all understand his request and, unable to disobey, surrender their wills to his and mount up behind him. Many have ridden with the dark man to fairyland; fewer have joined him on a homeward journey.

Mortals who return and, despite warnings, disclose fairy secrets or boast of newly acquired powers encounter again the dark, silent man. A fairy queen requires discretion from her former guests who, if they violate the terms of her hospitality, must suffer a reminder by her faithful servant. Efficiently he removes the offender's eye (and his fairy sight) or with a touch withers the muscles of an arm or leg. The errand accomplished, the dark man silently removes himself from his victim's presence.

The grey man or far liath appears as a fog and covers land and sea with his mantle. He obscures the rocks so that ships crash upon them and darkens the road so that travellers unwittingly stumble over precipices to their deaths. Because of him many a galleon was wrecked and many a mortal never returned home for dinner.

In times of famine the man of hunger or far gorta travels the roads, begging alms. Hardly a layer of flesh clings to his cheeks; and his arms, thin as stripped sticks, barely have the strength to proffer the alms cup. Even in winter, his rags scarcely cover his modesty. Some turn from him in dis-

70

gust; some, in their selfishness, avoid him; but all those who, despite the desperate times, freely give alms will be blessed forever with prosperous good luck.

Pooka

At night the pooka goes abroad, sometimes as an eagle flinging a man on his back and flying to the moon, sometimes as a black goat with wide wicked horns leaping on a mortal's shoulders and clinging with its claws until the man drops dead or blesses himself thrice. It is a bird, a bat, an ass, a solitary nightmare shape. Although it is an indistinct creature, like a dream dimly remembered yet arousing great fears, its flesh is warm, solid and palpable to the touch. Most often it appears as a terrible black horse, huge and sleek, breathing blue flames, with eyes of yellow fire, a snort like thunder, a smell like sulphur, a stride that clears mountains and a human voice deep as a cave. With a sound sometimes like the head-on crashing of trains, sometimes like the ripping of trees from the earth, it haunts rivers and frightens fishermen and sailors, shivering in their boats, fearful of approaching land. Sometimes it follows the ships to sea. Often at night the pooka lays pitfalls before horses' feet, taking a man up and riding him clear round the country at breakneck speed until he loses his grip and flies headlong into a bog ditch.

Yet for all its black deeds, the pooka now is a tame creature compared to what it was before Brian Ború curbed it. In ancient days the pooka was lord over all that went forth after dark, save those on errands of mercy. All roads belonged to it; and few who travelled them lived to tell. For the pooka kicked hard enough to pulverise human bones and could lift a man like an empty sack onto its back and jump with him into the sea, so deep that he drowned. Sometimes it sprang over a cliff and let the man, a bloody corpse,

71

tumble to the bottom. Satan's minister it was then and God save the poor sinner caught by the pooka on Hallowe'en Eve, for he would find himself in the midst of a witches' ring with his limbs torn from their sockets, and the fiends toasting his health with huge noggins of his blood.

But Brian Ború tamed it with a charm made from three hairs from a pooka's tail and thrown round its neck like a bridle. At the first pull, the hairs were transformed into threads of steel. Crossing himself and mounting, Brian Ború fiercely reined the beast and rode it until it heaved with exhaustion and promised never to kill another man save un-Irish blackguards. Since then it takes only drunkards on its madcap ridings, and always returns them to the ditch where it found them, no worse for some bruises and a drunken tale.

Now it avoids the highways, sticking to the footpaths, where a man with too many pints might stumble, but heroes such as Brian Ború hardly travel. Many precipices and caverns, places where a mortal might go astray in the night, are named after it. But now as always those who walk on God's path suffer no harm.

Dullahan

At dead of night a headless horseman rides wild upon a headless horse; wherever he stops a mortal dies. His face is the colour and texture of moulding cheese; his head, with his mouth making a bridge from ear to ear and its huge eyes darting like flies, lies firmly tucked beneath his arm. The head of his black horse with its flaming eyes and short-cropped ears outdistances its body by six yards or more. Such is the dullahan, a ghastly creature ever ready to fling a basin of blood at a healthy man's face.

Sometimes he, with the grey-haired banshee shrieking by his side, drives a black coach drawn by six black horses with tails sweeping the ground and not a head among them. Flickering candles set in the hollows of skulls light the way; thigh-bone spokes flash white as they turn; a man's spine serves as a pole; and a mildewed pall, well chewed by the worms, covers it all. Some say the dullahan is the devil's own man but surely he serves no master but Death.

In fear of the headless rider gates fly open; men alone in the fields at night cower behind the bushes because of his reputation with a whip. Since the dullahan has no head, some claim he cannot see, but nevertheless with a whip he accurately removes the eyes of all mortals presumptuous enough to spy on his ventures. Somewhat defective in seeing, the dullahan resents those who, from birth, have been skilled in the art.

A man once fell in with a company of dullahans, with their heads bobbing like balloons in sign of greeting. When they offered him a drink, he could hardly refuse; but as soon as he downed it his head flew off and went bobbing like the rest. In the morning it was attached as fast as ever to his neck, but the man remembered little of the affair for by virtue of the drink he had lost his head. Thoughts often tend to be truncated when a head departs from its body.

The dullahan has a number of cousins and headlessness seems to be a family trait. The Gan Ceann once followed a boat bound for America and would have overtaken it if a gold pin had not been dropped; for nothing puts fear in the creatures as fast as gold. Once a mortal chased a cloaked womanly figure through field and bog, but he had no luck in kissing her because of her want of a head.

Ghosts

Ghosts are not fairies; and fairyland is not Limbo. But a strange subtle link exists between them. Many of the solitary fairies are acquainted with Death, having accompanied him on his errands; therefore, opportunities have arisen for them to encounter his tenants. Some say the fairies draw forth a mortal soul, or ghost, from its dead body in order to secure it from the hands of Satan. The fairies' neutrality, they say, protects it until it arrives at Heaven's gate. Assuredly a soul which haunts the earth has not arrived at its proper post-mortem station, but resides temporarily in a twilight world, neither of heaven nor of earth. In this world, fairies are likely to be encountered. But, contrary to opinion, fairies do not play escort to souls nor have interest in coaxing them from their bodies. If ghosts spend some time in the twilight world, it is their own affair; and the fairies are not possessive. Sometimes the fairy friends and enemies have a mortal fight in the grave-yard over his soul. But they do so for the love of the fight, and in their battles forget the soul as it goes its own intended way. It may be that the corporeal insubstantiality of ghosts and fairies engenders an affinity, but more likely the affinity arises from mortal carelessness in lumping together all crea-tures who, unlike themselves, lack flesh.

It must be remembered that while ghosts often reside in fairyland, fairies never intrude upon either God's or Satan's dominions. Like Death, fairies are indifferent to good and evil; their lands therefore serve as a comfortable neutralia for those ghosts who have not yet made the commitment. Furthermore, ghosts and solitary fairies both take an inter-est in mortal affairs and possibly wish to exchange notes. Whatever the reasons, ghost frequently wander the elusive fields of fairyland; and on November Eve ghost and fairy join hands and dance in a wild, frenzied circle until the end of night.

Some falsely believe that ghosts—partly under fairy rules and partly under church punishment—haunt the earth as a penance for wrongs done to either fairy or church or both. But this view does justice neither to the good people nor to the church. Ghosts have their own reasons for sticking temporarily to earth. Some are held here by earthly longings, others by some unfulfilled duty or anger against the living. In former days when a man was displayed in the coffin, the living would turn back the toe ends of his socks with a pin. If the man were buried thus, he would come banging on all the doors and windows each evening until the coffin was unearthed and the pin removed. A woman who died came back nightly to care for her child. This she would have continued until the babe was weaned, but her brothers one night seized her round the waist and brought her back, permanently and intact, to life.

Some ghosts remain in a house because they are as comfortable there in death as in life. These house ghosts are always harmless; their acts are well intentioned and their presence guaranteed to bring good luck. The house will be tidied, the cows milked, and the hay harvested if a sentimental ghost abides in a home.

Sometimes a mortal stumbles upon a ghost conclave where he will see all the dead he has ever known. But he should avoid shaking hands with an old friend for the handclasp of a ghost burns like fire. Wherever a ghost touches mortal flesh, a black mark will be indelibly etched. Sometimes ghosts throw off the remnants of their flesh and dance naked in their bones, seizing available mortals as their partners. The wilder they dance the wilder they feel until the urge to battle overcomes them. Then they pull off their left arms and slash and strike lustily with their right. Since they are indiscriminate about their blows, a mortal should attempt immediate extrication and flight. Once a female ghost attacked a man she had sworn vengeance against, but he quickly threw a plough chain about her. Struggle as she would she could not get loose to harm him for the chain was blessed against such creatures as she. Recommendation: carry a plough chain whenever invited to a ghostly dance.

Ghosts are heard clanking and creaking about fairy forts. They often moan in graveyards. Some say that the last person to be buried has charge of all the souls and the maintenance of the peace of the grounds until the death of another releases it from its duty.

A woman might be alone at home and see through the window the very likeness of herself standing upon a hill. It is a fetch. If she sees it in the morning she is assured of long life; if in the evening, her life will be no longer than that of the turf block she has thrown in the fire. Unfortunately, the fetch of the evening more frequently appears. Every man and woman in Ireland has his own fetch; but most mortals, lacking the power to see them, are luckily unaware of their fate.

Fairy Animals

Many animals roam the fairy underlands and water resorts, and frequently they stray into mortal realms. Great steeds have charged nobly out of the sea, only to be entangled, panting and helpless, in a fisherman's net. Cows often rise up from the sea in search of sun-greened grass to feed their calves. On May Day especially, fairy cows appear and bring good luck to the farmer whose fields they cross. Rarely is a mortal every honoured, save on that day, by the Glas Gaivlen, the sacred milk-white cow studded with bright green spots. Wherever she treads the grass grows greener, the potato bigger and the hay more abundant.

Black cats and lake serpents guard the fairy treasure well. Cats, as legends have it, were once serpents and that is why they are so hard to kill and so dangerous to meddle with. Somnambulance and indestructability are excellent virtues in treasure warders; and hence both cats and serpents excel in their work.

The most predominant characteristic of fairy animals is their ability to defy natural laws. Cows breathe underwater; pigs appear and disappear at will. Trout and salmon converse with mortals in fluent Irish. Hares have been caught, washed, skinned and boiled, but never add a flavour to the soup; nor can a mortal sink his teeth in their flesh. A fairy trout when thrown in a pan will not brown, and has been known to leap from the fire and out the door in the form of a glimmering girl.

This leads to the question whether fairy animals are actually animals at all. The answer is complex. Some are known to be glamoured objects, such as the wisps of straw which become for a night great black steeds which cross a mountain at a single leap. A log looks and moans like a dying cow or woman. The fairies have even made an old nag so resemble a cow that its mortal owners, once they slew and prepared it, were convinced they were eating fresh beef.

Some are suspected to be fairies themselves who take on elusive animal forms to tease mortals; such are the appearing and disappearing hares which men may chase until doomsday but will never catch. Some animals, like the seal, are of an ambiguous nature, being part animal and part fairy man or woman. All seals are intimate with the fairies, but one is never sure if all, or only a few, are actually silkies.

Of course, mortal cows and sheep graze in fairyland, having been stolen from mortal realms to nourish the good people. Guarding cats and serpents are animals in their own fairy right. Quite a motley menagerie abides therefore in fairyland and occasionally haunts the mortal lands; and to say which kind is which is far too discriminating a task for a mortal.

IV

OF TIME AND PLACE

May Eve

During May Eve, known in ancient Ireland as the Beltaine (formerly a Druidic festival for the fire and sun god, Baal), fairies have the greatest power over the things of this earth. No man, woman or child should venture from home lest they become permanent residents of fairyland. Flowers should be affixed to the windows of homes so that fairies might not enter and take hold of desirable mortals. Sheep, goats and cows should be locked within doors, with all the appropriate protective aids of primroses, holy water and fire about the animals to ward off fairy powers.

On May Eve fairies are in their best humour. They feel the spring as, if not more, intensely than we do, and thus celebrate it with sprightly song and dancing. Every hawthorn tree has a fairy band disporting in rings about it. Every road resounds with their feet, every field with their calling. The Glas Gaivlen, the fairy cow with green spots, graces the farmers' fields and brings them luck.

With great vitality the fairies rejoice in their eternal youth and beauty, seeking, too, mortals capable of joining them in their joy. On May Eve they seek and celebrate beauty; but being in such good spirits, they frequently take pleasure in an old crone or withered man and thus in their amusement spirit them away. A mortal who would find the good people had best search the raths and hawthorn trees on May Eve; and whoever dances to the fairy pipes and returns gains such agility and grace that to his dying day he will be king of dancers.

On May Day several precautions should be taken, for if a spell is placed cn that day its power lasts until the next May Eve. Neither fire nor water should be given out of the house that day or else the turf might not burn nor the water rise up from the well. A large fire should be made and not allowed to die down, for the smoke is repugnant to the good people. Never lend a churn or dishes to your neighbour on that day or your butter will somehow appear in her churn. In fact, just before sunrise on May Day the fairies are quite apt to take all the butter out of the milk, if the churn and the cows are not properly guarded. It is always wise to forestall the good people by pouring out some of the milk as an offering before they arrive.

Although May Eve is most subject to fairy influence, fairies consider all the month of May their special time. No mortal at any time should doze by a fairy rath unless he desires to encounter the *sidhe*; but in the month of May he should avoid sleeping anywhere in the open air. A day-time snooze may turn into a seven-year adventure. Fairies do most of their travelling in May and hence are quite aware of human happenings. They are given to resting by lakes and streams where they net and capture solitary mortals wandering in the secluded places. Many are taken, and most who appear to die in the month of May, especially children and beautiful women, are actually healthy and alive in the land of the *sidhe*.

Midsummer's Eve

On the evening of 23 June, bonfires are lit throughout Ireland. Each village greets the night with a bright blaze; and every city is ringed with fires lit in its surrounding lands. Fiddlers, pipers and concertinists play up the old tunes as the people dance round the fire. A night of great merriment it is, but few know more of the event save that it is called bonfire night and is the eve of St John's Day. Before the christian conversion in Ireland, the peasantry kindled bonfires only on the eve of May, the time most sacred to fairies. Fearing the fairy power of that eve, St Patrick transferred the holiday to the saint's protection. He ordered the fires traditionally lit in May to be set in honour of St John the Baptist—a figure eminently more respectable than any disporting fairy.

Accordingly the people changed bonfire night to Midsummer's Eve; but, despite the saints, the people adhered to their more ancient beliefs. For generations on this Eve, men, women and children, carrying brands of fire, leaped or walked through the fire to claim its power for a year against fairy and other occult forces. A man about to depart on a long journey jumped backwards and forwards three times across a well fed fire to ensure a successful undertaking. A young man about to wed did so to purify himself for the marriage state. Whoever wished to undertake some hazardous enterprise leaped to secure invulnerability. As the fire sunk low young girls skipped across to procure good husbands, while pregnant women carefully walked over it to ensure a happy delivery. Cattle were led across to prevent their milk from running dry. Fire, the greatest of fairy preventatives, thus protected mortals and their animals for another year.

The fairies were never fooled by the change in date; they still held their May powers even when the church denied them. Midsummer meant nothing to them save as another pleasant night among many to delight in. Only to the Amadawn or fool did June become sacrosanct as he blundered about the island, devastating mortals with his mind-debilitating touch.

Today on Midsummer's Eve, the Irish remember neither the fairies nor the saints. They are content with an evening's innocent amusement. It is small wonder that the higher powers have deserted us, if we are so easily satisfied with a few sticks of wood and a pleasant flash of red.

November Eve

November Eve is the gloomiest of the fairy festivals, the lightsome fairy power being overshadowed by that of death and the devil. It is Samnhain Eve, the feast of the moon, when Druids were wont to pour out libations to propitiate evil spirits and spirits of the dead. It is the festival of darkness and secretive light. Witches cast their spells; the pooka lustily remembers its former pact with the devil. In stupid glee it leaps over the land, despoiling the blackberries. In the name of the devil, young girls lay the table with food in hopes that the fetch of their future lover may come through the window, eat of their viands and thus bind a love pact. The dead arise; and, when not battling with their bones, they join hands with the fairies in a frantic whirling step. The fairies love the intensity of the dance and the night, but the party is not all their own; the evening's style therefore is uncomfortably unfairylike.

Yet the fairies hold their own amongst the more sinister powers; contact with death and the devil reminds them of old vengeances and irritates old wounds. They might blight the family and crops of a man who built his house too near their fort or attack with greater fury than usual a mortal who walked innocently upon their paths. In their haste to arrive at the feasting place they sometimes beat a path through a house, blighting the children within and the cattle without.

The evening's highlights, for the fairies, are the rousing battles, the clattering of their swords and their shouts of mock-vengeance as each faction fights its neighbour. The great Ulster, Munster, Leinster and Connaught fairy tribes lock arms. Often they fight to claim that year's soon-to-be-harvested potato crop. The cry 'Black potatoes, black potatoes, we'll have then now' rings through the thundering storms and rains of that night.

Tír-na-n-Óg

Tír-na-n-Óg is the land of perpetual youth, where those who reside, fairy and former mortal alike, luxuriate in all that is new and beautiful and will never die. The old Irish gods, Lugh of the silver spear and golden arm, the Daghda of the great cauldron that gives life to the dead and food to the living, Mananán Mac Lir of the waves and Angus Óg, the Apollo-like god of love and poetry, all eat the golden apples of the land and converse with the great Irish heroes—Cuchulain, Conchobar, Finn MacCumhail, Connla—all who spent in battle joys.

Tír-na-n-Óg is known by many names, for all who know it see it differently, each according to his or her own qualities. Being the land of the heart's desire, it has as many forms as the world has desires. Thrice fifty isles are said to lie west of Ireland, each affording a different delight. For some, Tír-na-n-Óg is May Mell, the Plain of Pleasures; for the more competitive, Mag Mon, the Plain of Sports. It is Tír Tairngiri, Land of Promise, and Tír-na-Sorcha, Land of Light. In times of national disaster it appears to the Irish people as Hy Brazil, the Isle of the Blest, the land of the great heroes, its appearance reminding those alive of ancient deeds and encouraging them to live true to the ancestral blood.

Tír-na-n-Óg is everywhere and nowhere definite, but most often it is beneath the waters, for life in the deeps is unaffected by time. When the lake or sea waters are low and clear, the tops of towers and stately buildings in multifarious colours may be seen. A mortal once dived into the waters until they parted and found himself on dry land, with a sky and a sun above just like ours. The land was a

82

huge pleasure garden where gods, fairies and former mortals took their ease and spoke of great days past and to come. Beneath the waters the inhabitants of Tír-na-n-Óg idle and make love; on earth they war. The warrior Daniel O'Donoghue keeps a fine retinue of warlike youths and maidens underneath the waters of Lochlein near Killarney, ready at a moment to rise up and fight Ireland's oppressors.

Sometimes Tír-na-n-Óg is a paradisal island afloat upon still waters, appearing and vanishing like a mirage to sailors. St Brendan set sail for it on Atlantic waters, convinced it was to be found and abundant with the blessings of God. On clear days it can be seen from the western-most cliffs of Ireland, but it always recedes before those who sail out to find it. A sea-battered crew once saw the land of the heart's desire, but it vanished at their approach until they shot at it with an arrow barbed with hot steel. The arrow stuck fast: the fire burned the land clean of illusion and so the men found it, stationary, inhabited and rich in ethereal and corporeal beauties.

Many have set out to find the magic land; a rare few are invited. If a damsel seems to walk on music and bears in her hand a silver-leafed apple branch, be sure she is a denizen of that world come to lure you to where the wood does not decay and all creatures sport naked about the bushes without sin or shame. A curragh propelled solely by your desire will conduct you to her home, where she will clasp you eternally to her snowfair body.

A sensuous paradise is Tír-na-n-Óg. All that is voluptuous, serene and complete, celebrates its existence there. Skies never blacken above it; shyly waves caress its shores. The furious elements of storm and drought and blight respect its borders and go their ways. A sacred well founded by Prince Connla renews all who drink from it; and the earth herself reveals her love for her inhabitants by appearing forever in her true, ever-young, ever-fertile form. In these congenial surroundings, gods and former mortals rejoice

83

with each other, hunting together and sporting and feasting and making love. Whatever they embrace exults; whatever they eat or drink delights them, leaving no sense of satiety.

All who are intense in their desire are at home in Tír-na-n-Óg. But mortals are a fickle crew; give them paradise and they will exchange it for hunger, strife and death. Those of us who would live in fairyland must learn to be content with perfection.

THE BOOK OF IRISH CURSES
By Patrick C. Power

The Book of Irish Curses is an extremely interesting, well written, fascinating and entertaining book. It is a remarkable blend of history, forklore and anecdote. The author deals at length with the types of Irish curses, their age and styles, their rituals, and concludes with a do-it-yourself cursing kit.

IN MY FATHER'S TIME
By Eamon Kelly

In My Father's Time invites us to a night of storytelling by Ireland's greatest and best loved *seanchaí*, Eamon Kelly. The fascinating stories reveal many aspects of Irish life and character. There are tales of country customs; matchmaking, courting, love; marriage and the dowry system; emigration, American wakes and returned emigrants. The stream of anecdotes never runs dry and the humour sparkles and illuminates the stories.

FABLES AND LEGENDS OF IRELAND
By Maureen Donegan

These tales were told and retold by word of mouth and, although they are full of magical creatures and enchanted castles, they are also about people: real people who suffered from indigestion and jealousy, just as we do. The Fianna, larger than life and swashbuckling across Ireland even into fairy cities beyond the sea, still live on, in spirit if not in the flesh, in an Ireland which is much changed since giants and heroes strode across it.

THE FIRST BOOK OF IRISH MYTHS AND LEGENDS
By Eoin Neeson

THE SECOND BOOK OF IRISH MYTHS AND LEGENDS
By Eoin Neeson

These two books contain a fascinating collection of tales and legends of Irish heroes.

IRISH COUNTRY PEOPLE
Kevin Danaher

Irish Country People is simply one fascinating glorious feast of folklore and interesting sidelights of history recorded without a fraction of a false note or a grain of sentimentality. The topics covered in the twenty essays range over a wide field of history, folklore, mythology and archaeology. There are discussions about cures, curses and charms; lords, labourers and wakes; names, games and ghosts; prayers and fairy-tales. Nowadays we find it hard to visualise the dark winter evenings of those times when there was no electric light, radio, television or cinemas. We find it harder to realise that such evenings were not usually long enough for the games, singing, card-playing, music, dancing and story-telling that went on.

We can read about a six-mile traffic jam near Tailteann in the year 1168, just before the Norman invasion, and the incident is authenticated by a reference to the *Annals of the Four Masters*. The whole book is tinged with quiet humour: 'You should always talk to a dog in a friendly, mannerly way, but you should never ask him a question directly, for what would you do if he answered you, as well he might?'

THE PLEASANT LAND OF IRELAND
Kevin Danaher

This book is well illustrated and gives a comprehensive picture of a way of life which though in great part is vanishing is still familiar to many of our countrymen.

LETTERS OF AN IRISH PARISH PRIEST
John B. Keane

There is a riot of laughter in every page and its theme is the correspondence between a country parish priest and his nephew who is studying to be a priest. Father O'Mora has been referred to by one of his parishioners as one who 'is suffering from an overdose of racial memory aggravated by religious bigotry.' John B. Keane's humour is neatly pointed, racy of the soil and never forced. This book gives a picture of a way of life which though in great part is vanishing is still familiar to many of our countrymen who still believe 'that priests could turn them into goats.' It brings out all the humour and pathos of Irish life. It is hilariously funny and will entertain and amuse everyone.

LETTERS OF A MATCHMAKER
John B. Keane

These are the letters of a country matchmaker faithfully recorded by John B. Keane, whose knowledge of matchmaking is second to none.

In these letters is revealed the unquenchable, insatiable longing that smoulders unseen under the mute, impassive faces of our batchelor brethren.

Comparisons may be odious but readers will find it fascinating to contrast the Irish matchmaking system with that of the 'Cumangettum Love Parlour' in Philadelphia. They will meet many unique characters from the Judas Jennies of New York to Finnuala Crust of Coomasahara who buried two giant-sized, sexless husbands but eventually found happiness with a pint-sized jockey from North Cork.

LETTERS OF A LOVE-HUNGRY FARMER
John B. Keane

John B. Keane has introduced a new word into the English language — 'chastitute'. This is the story of a chastitute, i.e. a man who has never lain down with a woman for reasons which are fully disclosed within this book. It is the tale of a lonely man who will not humble himself to achieve his heart's desire, whose need for female companionship whines and whimpers throughout. Here are the hilarious sex escapades of John Bosco McLane culminating finally in one dreadful deed.

LETTERS OF AN IRISH PUBLICAN
John B. Keane

In this book we get a complete picture of life in Knockanee as seen through the eyes of a publican, Martin MacMeer. He relates his story to his friend Dan Stack who is a journalist. He records in a frank and factual way events like the cattle fair where the people 'came in from the hinterland with caps and ash-plants and long coats', and the cattle stood 'outside the doors of the houses in the public streets.'

Through his remarkable perception we 'get a tooth' for all the different characters whom he portrays with sympathy, understanding and wit. We are overwhelmed by the charms of the place where at times 'trivial incidents assume new proportions.' These incidents are exciting, gripping, hilarious, touching and uncomfortable.

Send us your name and address if you would like to receive
our complete catalogue of books of Irish Interest.

THE MERCIER PRESS
4 Bridge Street, Cork, Ireland